Imogen
in Waiting

a memoir of modern reproduction

by Lindsay Bartels

THIRD RAIL PRESS

IMOGEN IN WAITING: A MEMOIR OF MODERN REPRODUCTION

Published by:
THIRD RAIL PRESS LLC
P.O. Box 20285
Albuquerque, NM 87154
www.thirdrailpress.org

Paperback ISBN: 979-8-9912123-8-0
Ebook ISBN: 979-8-9912123-9-7

"In *Imogen in Waiting*, Lindsay Bartels writes beautifully about a terribly hard decision. From the first page, Bartels plunges into her story, bringing readers along for each ache and triumph, every decision and crossroads. This book is a testament to science, maternal love, and the ineffable magic of intuition and connection beyond our understanding."

– Christie Tate, *New York Times* bestselling author of *Group*

"Luminous and wise, *Imogen* is a story for all women finding their path through motherhood and its many unpredictable challenges. From breast cancer to IVF to elementary school classrooms, Lindsay navigates the unknown time and again—and shows us all what it means to listen to our truth. A breathless read."

– Jessica Zucker, PhD, author of *Normalize It*

"As much as a memoir of body-in-crisis, this is also a memoir of big-hearted love, palpable on every page. Urgent, poetic, and wise, Lindsay's story is a shining light of resilience even in the face of the kind of tough choices that no young woman should face. I don't say this often, but *Imogen in Waiting* is an inspiring book."

– Lee Kofman, author of *The Writer Laid Bare*

"A moving, original, and tenderly-written work. This book is a gift—I couldn't put it down."

– Ariane Beeston, author of *Because I'm Not Myself, You See*

"Lindsay Bartels shows us that there are as many questions around motherhood as there are people. Intimate and fast-paced, *Imogen in Waiting* is a powerful investigation into motherhood in all of its manifestations."

– Ruthie Ackerman, author of *The Mother Code*

"Lindsay Bartels writes about her journey with the BRCA1 gene with a steady aim, moving fluidly between intellectualizing the science and grounding us in the body, while occasionally slipping into worlds where the mysterious and even the unknown seem to hold court. Bartels makes clear that navigating genetic illness is never simple—but also that we don't have to do it alone."

– Joselin Linder, author of *The Family Gene*

"*Imogen in Waiting* is an epic journey through the complexities of love and procreation in the face of unexpected challenges. It raises philosophical questions about the ethics of choice and leaves us wondering whether knowing too much serves or undermines enlivenment. A brave and moving story."

– Joanne Fedler, author of *Bring Us Home from Sorrow*

For my dad, with tremendous love.

c o v e r   n o t e

The artwork for the cover is a custom piece designed specifically for Lindsay's story by Jamie Kushner Blicher, an ink-on-paper artist who creates abstract works using unused IVF syringes donated by women around the world.

Since 2016, Jamie has been using her one-of-a-kind art to bring peace, joy, and beauty to those on infertility journeys. Visit www.glitterenthusiast.com to see more of the infertility stories, like this one, that she has so beautifully rendered on paper.

The opinions in this memoir are entirely my own, depicting my path and perspective; everyone's experience is unique. Yet I hope it helps every reader know it is always okay to stand up for your truth. Finding out more information is often more empowering than anticipated, and you can always change your mind.

Imogen
in Waiting

D ear Imogen,

This is the whole story.

The story of you,
your presence in our family,
and all the moments
no one knows,

except for your father and me.

Love,
Mom

The year is 2009.

I am twenty-six years old and live in San Francisco. I moved here on a premeditated whim, if that makes sense. I'd answered a silent call of sorts—something that pulled at my insides from the outside for a few years until I couldn't ignore it any longer. Much like you, Imogen.

After graduating with a bachelor's degree in filmmaking in Boulder, Colorado, and then giving that life a shot in the film mecca of Los Angeles, I gave in to the first real whisper of something nonsensical that called to me. Nonsensical meaning a leap without a safety net in place. I didn't have a job or know many people in San Francisco, but it invigorated me creatively and made me feel alive, and that, at the time, was enough for me.

Things fell into place like I knew they would. "Like attracts like," I had written as my senior quote in my high school yearbook. Like Bryan Adams' words—"Whatever the conscious mind thinks and believes, the subconscious identically creates"— or my mother's daily dialogue about reincarnation and otherworldliness, by 2009, it is happening. I'm making enough money in digital production—websites, motion graphics, etc.—

to live on my own, I have a growing group of interesting and successful friends, and I enjoy a very pleasant commute by foot: down from Pacific Heights, up through Nob Hill, and into Jackson Square. I go for a run around Alta Plaza Park most mornings and across the Golden Gate Bridge and back on Saturdays, followed by brunch with friends over copious amounts of Blue Bottle coffee.

I am also a year into dating Mark.

This is the first relationship I've had where I feel like I can be myself, effortlessly. A creative, intelligent light in me is matched in a way I don't have to fight for or explain. He is from South Africa, with a wonderfully unique-to-me accent, blue-gray eyes that harbor a twinkling smile, and a generous laugh. I love being in his orbit. Best of all, he is comfortable in his own skin, begetting the same in me.

Marriage isn't something Mark and I have even discussed, but things between us are growing. I recently saw a psychic in Corte Madera who told me, "He, with eyes like the sea, wants your hand in marriage." Weird, and kind of cool. She also told me I will have two children, maybe three. And that I'll live by the ocean and possibly take up surfing.

The water is too cold to surf in here, and maybe one day Mark will take me out in a wetsuit, but for now, we have our sights set on a trip to South Africa for his sister's wedding. We'll visit his hometown of Port Elizabeth for the festivities, then his family's holiday home on a river inland from Jeffrey's Bay, a special place he grew up escaping to, with his brothers, sister, and ninety-year-old gran.

It is two months out from this trip that a foreign entity interrupts the momentum I am having with life.

It quietly draws in all of my attention, this lump on the right side of my breast. A trapped marble that seemingly appeared overnight. I discover it when working late one night, stressing over what, at the time, I put way too much anxiety into: a banner ad for Commonwealth Bank.

Why am I hunched over my laptop at home, waiting and scratching the side of my chest, at 12:30 in the morning? Perhaps we are on a tight deadline; that is probably it. But what, exactly, am I waiting for? Whatever it is—a rendering from the artist or some coding from our engineer—I have to review it to make sure it works before I send it to the client.

Imogen, we are not saving lives here, that is for sure.

But in this moment, little do I know, I am saving my own. And that will become my new momentum that will lead me to you.

Like attracts like.

part I | *before you*

1 | shoes

I'm lying down. I don't remember if I am on a chair or a table nor can I give you a wide-lens view of the room. I'm very much there with my head supported, looking off to the left. To the right is the doctor, in scrubs, who I haven't met prior to this appointment. This is my biopsy.

"Oh, it is probably just a cyst from your cycle," someone close to me said—someone who cared and didn't want me to worry. But I had a sense that this foreign entity inside me was abnormal and the sooner I got answers, the better.

An ultrasound determined the lump did not have liquid in it—was *not* a cyst—and, in sync with this knowing deep inside me, was not nothing, which brought me here.

"I'm going to numb the area," the doctor narrates.

Surgical instruments clang and a topical cream is applied.

I immediately told Mark. He has a wonderful way about him of being present that I haven't come across in most Americans. He genuinely listens with no ulterior motives.

Insisting he come over the evening after my discovery, an otherwise happy and healthy 5'4" me sat on his lap and directed his hand under my arm, into my shirtsleeve, to feel the lump.

"It's hard, right?" I said. "And weird?"

"My sister gets these things all the time," he said, "and they always turn out to be nothing. It's probably nothing."

I think of his sister and, again, how this isn't quite nothing, when I notice more than two physicians hovering at my right side.

"Now you will hear a sound like a staple gun," the doctor says.

The sound is jarring. Loud. It passes, and then I'm done.

All this waiting has felt stretched out like endless taffy, with uncertainty folding over more uncertainty. It's been over six weeks since that night I was working so late. The closer I get to any concrete information, the more my nerves get the better of me and trigger fear-wrenched sobs when I'm alone. The fear tries to envelop me. But if I keep moving, I know I'll get to where I need to be—a place where this sensation can compress into answers.

As I change back into my clothing, I think about Mark and our upcoming trip to South Africa and how I really want to go. On our second date, he mentioned his family's home on the river, its basic concrete structure, the recently installed plumbing—and how he grew up comfortable among the sounds and movements of the trees, the water, the dark. There was a quiet question in him feeling out if I could handle a space with that kind of isolation, that kind of rhythm with nature.

I am eager to prove myself his equal, to stand on the kikuyu grass and hear the birds in the wattle trees beside the lapping current—echoes of the family videos he often shares with me— and experience this connection that causes him to take in a more expansive sensory catalog of his surroundings than I do.

We are supposed to fly out in two weeks' time.

Once I'm dressed and have my things, I stop by the front desk to ask the receptionist when they will send me the results.

"You should receive them in four to five business days," she says, then backtracks, "but with Thanksgiving coming up, you may not hear until the following week."

That's not as soon as I'd hoped, but as I zip up my coat to exit the building, it feels promising that I'll still be able to get on that flight and be done with all this ambiguity.

Imogen, I need to tell this story so that I can imagine you in my shoes—these shoes that are now on my feet. I don't really want to look at them. Do you? They're not the ruby slippers I'm used to. But I have them, which means that you just might have them too—and I can't take them off or shake them off or ignore them.

I must move forward with them on.

2 | well, fuck

Back in Los Angeles, I never felt like any of my work peers—of all ages and generations—were particularly grown up. They all still acted childlike—wanting to belong, wanting to find an in into the industry, or sitting on the sidelines waiting to be chosen to play. Those already in the field, or close to it, gave their lives to filmmaking. Ate, drank, slept film. And that recipe for success wasn't something that aligned with me.

Here in SF, I've found myself among those living a more balanced approach. People here lean into their creative drives in addition to having families and separate interests. I'm not saying they are the gold standard in *how* it should be done, necessarily, as late nights tend to be the norm—along with sacrifices at certain points—but I am taking note, seeing them trying to find their way, seeing if it suits my own.

My boss and executive producer, Jan, is a petite but big-hearted woman who makes time for anyone and everyone who walks through her door, while being impeccably *on it*. A mom to two of her own growing children, she makes our office feel like a family away from our families.

The morning after I found the lump, I told Jan and she quickly wrote out her gynecologist's name and number on a sticky note for me so I could see someone here, now. I got an appointment with her doctor's nurse practitioner for a few days out rather than waiting for one at my father's practice in Colorado with his physician assistant. This helped me move things along, like I knew I needed to do, and feel like I wasn't alone or so far from home.

Now it is the Tuesday after Thanksgiving, and a call comes through my direct line. I share an office with the company's creative director—a tall, gregarious windsurfer with wavy white-blond hair who we call Rowan. He is much more senior to me, a father to a daughter, and always happy to lend a hand and throw some encouragement my way whenever I'm navigating new trenches. We've recently been paired up in this space together and share an easy cadence.

The day is crisp, the sky a clear, vibrant blue. The winter holidays are around the corner. The sun streams in through our window above Battery Street, and my hand passes through it to the handset when I pick up.

"This is Lindsay," I say into the black rectangular mouthpiece, expecting a client on the other end.

"Hi, Lindsay, do you have a moment?" says a voice I do not recognize. "This is one of the nurses from CPMC."

"Yes," I say, my heart pounding. She can't give me a cancer diagnosis over the phone, surely?

"We've received the results of your biopsy," she jumps right in, "and it is cancerous…"

WHAT?! my insides scream as my pulse elevates.

"We'd like you to come in today. How soon can you come in? We're here until 4 p.m. Do you have someone who can come with you?"

Mark will come with me, I think, as I try to catch up with my racing thoughts. "Yes, yes, I'll be there," I tell her.

"We'll be expecting you." She hangs up.

"Fuck!" I say out loud, staring motionless, in shock, at the innocuous piece of plastic I am still holding. Rowan turns to me.

"What was that?" he says.

"I was just told I have cancer." I set down the receiver and stand up, frozen in place, as Rowan too pushes his chair away from his desk and stands. He crosses the few feet between us and puts his arms around me. I appreciate this so much. "You'll get through this, Lindsay. My girlfriend had a breast cancer scare. She has a really good doctor. I'll text you her name."

Did I tell him about the lump? Did I say breast *cancer?* I can't recall as I thank him, not quite believing I'll actually need his girlfriend's doctor's name.

The absurdity of this information hasn't yet sunk in.

But I know I have an appointment to get to and, as a doer, that is something I can do. I walk down the hall to my boss's office, step inside, and shut the door. My heart is hammering.

Jan sees me and stills her typing, giving me her full attention.

"I got my biopsy results," I say. I glance down at my hands. They're shaking. "It's cancer. I have to go talk to them. *Soon. Today.*"

Jan is steady, calm. She schedules a cab to meet me outside the building. It will arrive in half an hour.

When I meet Mark outside the medical center, I take note of the name on the exterior wall in front of us: Breast Health. I hesitate, not wanting any labels to define me, not wanting the fear that has returned palpably around me to penetrate who I am. But people inside these sliding doors are expecting me, so I move up the steps into the building.

Once I check in, we are quickly ushered into a room. We sit

in chairs at a round table and a nurse—yes, a nurse—sits across from us. I can't find my voice to ask her where the doctors are. I have an elephant on my chest—a sensation I've only felt in dreams—that I can't shake. Within moments, the piling of bricks begins:

"Here are the pathology results of your biopsy," the nurse says. She places a sheet in front of me full of boxes with numbers that make no sense. She points to the first box. "The mass measures a little over two centimeters across. About the size of your thumbnail. The size puts you in Stage II cancer."

Stage II does not sound good, I think, keeping still, as images of a female protagonist in an old '80s movie flash through my head, where she is doubled over, crippled by her cancer. *How did this happen so fast?*

"On a scale of one to three," she points to the adjacent box, "with three being the worst, your cancer is a three for how fast the cells are multiplying."

Well, fuck.

Her finger then rests on the third box. It reads "no hormone receptors detected." I try to understand what that could possibly mean, but before I can ask, she continues.

"Your cancer is called triple negative breast cancer."

Oh my gosh, quit saying cancer! I want to scream as I try to process all of the information.

"You will need to have a lumpectomy. You will likely need chemotherapy and radiation; your hair will probably fall out. You will receive medications to keep you from being nauseous, and with radiation, you'll need special creams and care because it will burn your skin."

Her eyes lock on mine in a gaze I don't want to hold but do. *Why is she going through every thinkable scenario right now?*

I want to tune her out. She isn't my doctor—isn't even a doctor at all—but she keeps the weight coming.

"You will need to have more tests. You need to meet with doctors right away since this is an aggressive cancer and needs to be treated immediately. Clear your schedule."

I stare at her, shell-shocked.

"Have you thought of fertility preservation? You will also need to see an infertility specialist before you undergo chemotherapy…"

She places sheets of information, one on top of the other, into a folder that thickens with the air in the room.

An angry heat boils inside me toward this nurse. *Why is she the one telling me all this?*

Mark remains beside me in silence. I have no idea what is going through his mind, as I try to cope with what this all means.

My eyes shift away to the wall and I blink them closed. Forget the bricks; I feel like I've been hit by a bus. It seems as if I was going about my life blissfully unaware in one direction—and now, suddenly, I'm here, paralyzed by this moment.

A voice in my head reminds me to breathe, that this is not necessarily how it will all go down. I think of our plans for South Africa and how I won't make the wedding. *Will Mark go anyway?* I wonder. Why is this the thing that makes me the saddest right now?

An image of Mark and I sharing that memory together slips through my vision when the angel that is Carol enters and nurse what's-her-name leaves the room.

Carol is a volunteer. She is patient and instantly exudes compassion and kindness. She speaks softly, slowly, like a balm, telling us she, too, had breast cancer and will sit with me to go through these lists and will schedule my first appointments for me.

She explains that, like today, it'll be helpful to have someone with me at these appointments moving forward—another ear, a scribe, support. I look at Mark and don't know how much has sunk in for him, how much he even *wants* to absorb, or if he is, like me, unable to move and grateful Carol is here.

"There will be a lot of information and a lot to do—and, Lindsay, you will do it," she says encouragingly, finding my eyes to make sure I've heard her.

I nod. Her warmth slowly brings me back to life—with a certainty that I will see this through.

Later, we have dinner plans.

It is cold out and I huddle close to Mark at the entry of a crowded trendy restaurant while we wait for our table. A faint glow of light caresses the faces of couples on dates and colleagues recalling their day with laughter.

"It feels so strange to be among this normalcy," I whisper. "What are other people going through?" I look up and catch the sorrow in his eyes that matches my own. "You just don't know, do you?"

My phone pings. It's a text from Rowan with the name of his girlfriend's doctor. It is the same one Carol set me up with.

"Oh, wow." I show Mark. "This makes me feel a little better. A vote of confidence."

I sigh and Mark opens a panel of his navy peacoat, inviting me in. He pulls the wool around me, kissing my head as it lands on his chest. I stand there, sinking into the security of his embrace, feeling like an impostor for the first time in the effervescence of life, missing the carefree old me, as the restaurant activity swirls around us.

3 | acute and immediate

My first appointment the next morning is with the fertility preservation specialist. Fertility happens to be my father's field of expertise and a subject I never anticipated confronting so quickly out of college (or ever, honestly). My mother is only able to fly in from Colorado tomorrow evening to be with me. Work resumes, understandably, for Mark—the CFO of a growing start-up—so Jan accompanies me to this appointment, to be that extra ear.

On our walk from the parking lot into the building, Jan asks, "How are you doing, Lindsay?"

I don't reveal to her that I'm bummed about the wedding. That trip has veered so far out of my orbit that to recall it, I would have to shift the entirety of my energy backward and that feels too gloomy to fathom. I'm more frustrated that I can't fast-forward away what is blaringly in front of me, in order to get back to the trajectory I was on before. That I don't have that kind of power.

"I feel like I'm just now finding my feet," I say instead, processing my feelings at the same time. "I like being independent and not relying on anyone. The most challenging thing for me about this moment, for better or worse," I laugh, "is that I have to switch gears—and I…" I sigh. "I don't like that I have to stop and ask for help. Especially with something so personal and out of my control."

Truly, she is the world's best of bosses—successful, available, and caring. I admire her mentorship of others and here she is, setting aside all of her mounting responsibilities to be with me.

Jan wraps an arm around my waist and pulls me into her hip as we walk. "People want to help you, Lindsay," she says, sharing a smile. "It gives them something to do when they don't know what else to do." She stops walking and turns her face to mine, bracing her hands on my shoulders so I hear her. "I want to be here. I am happy to be here."

In the fertility preservation doctor's office, we sit next to each other in the two chairs in front of his desk, naive as to what to expect. We share a nervous anticipation disguised by well-practiced professionalism.

Immediately, without having seen a breast surgeon or oncologist, the doctor puts me on a schedule and protocol—with Jan as my witness—for an egg retrieval within two weeks. My ovaries will be stimulated to produce an atypical number of eggs, which will then be surgically extracted, frozen, and stored in their lab.

I'm not asked if I'd like this choice. It is just what is done, as a cancer patient, to keep me moving forward.

"To give you childbearing options," I'm told, "because your fertility may not come back after chemo."

But I don't even know if I need chemo yet! I want to shout, but I nod and stare instead—because I've never had to face these kinds of options in this sort of time crunch before.

It is very strange to find myself in this position at a time not of my choosing. Until now, I've only thought of protecting myself from pregnancy—how much I *don't* want to get pregnant and wish to find my own creative life independently first. I've hardly had the opportunity to take my fertility for granted.

Growing up, I never imagined myself having babies as a life goal, or even an end goal to a relationship. I believed in romance and enjoyed happily-ever-after stories, but they were background fodder, magic to fuel the main event. That main event being something vast, inclusive of connection and adventure, that I could share with a special someone—only after which I imagined children would come.

"Does your boyfriend want to fertilize your eggs?" the doctor asks.

"Huh?" I say, trying to come back to reality. My cheeks heat when I remember my boss here, listening.

Upon seeing my blank face, he tags on, "You can decide the day of. He will just need to be present to contribute a sperm sample."

Gosh, how am I even going to have this conversation with Mark? We haven't gone there yet in our discussions about "us." Our relationship feels steady, but we operate from a day-at-a-time kind of mentality, mostly because I don't want to add any unnecessary pressure.

These outside forces are speeding things up. How much is solid between us? Can we withstand being catapulted into the future like this?

The doc tells me I need to come back tomorrow—to pick up my medications, learn how to administer them, and to please bring said boyfriend so we can sign some legal paperwork, just in case.

"But!" I finally raise my hand. "I haven't even met with my doctor or doctors yet about next steps. Are they going to be okay with me doing this first?"

I honestly can't remember what he says other than he is doing his job—protecting my fertility in the window of time he knows he has for certain: now—before anyone else can say differently.

He goes on to reiterate that *if* I have chemo, it is not guaranteed that my ovarian function will return. What is left could be a deserted wasteland, egg-wise. So, basically, he is trying to make the best of this moment in the face of more uncertainty ahead.

Even though I haven't been here before, he assures me that he has.

It is all so much, Imogen. Too much already that I wouldn't wish on anyone. *That I wouldn't wish on anyone.* I have to say it again. Because I forget this. It was all *that* jarring. That acute and immediate.

I type more appointments in my phone calendar and am handed another folder full of papers. Somewhere deep down, I know I am being rooted for—that this push through the next door is what I need, but so much feels out of my hands and compounds the discomfort I have of letting others do what is best for me. *I* want to do what is best for me but can't even catch up with what that is right now. It's like the reins in creating my own life have been handed over. I want them back desperately.

I say goodbye to Jan, thank her, then walk home and call my dad.

He tells me that he knows of the fertility preservation specialist I've just seen. He's met the head of my new doc's department, who he has often asked questions of at conferences and valued her research.

That's reassuring, I think, as he goes on to share that it does sound like it could be helpful to retrieve some eggs now. He gets the logic behind it, for those who don't have a partner.

"But," he points out, "the research there is still emerging and it is not guaranteed eggs will be useful after being frozen. What is more commonly practiced and research-driven for future options is freezing embryos."

Hmm. I hang up, not so reassured after all.

That evening, I share with Mark the many pieces that have been set in motion. Discussions we aren't ready to face emerge in full presence, demanding attention, pulling at us for desires that haven't yet formed.

It is uncomfortable for me to put myself out there like this, asking if Mark will make embryos with me, especially when I don't know what *I* want. I am desperate to manifest answers only to find that those hidden vessels inside both of us are, well, empty.

Our hearts aren't invested yet in this stage of life, so our heads are trying to wrap around the best way forward. The most logical way. But it is breaking my heart in the process because I don't want to have to demand this of Mark and yet, here I am, putting him on the spot and getting a blank face in return.

Thoughts continue to bang around in my head before bed, knocking any free will down with them: *Will I ever be able to have kids? What if this is the only option? But I don't want to have kids now! Mark doesn't seem to want to either. Will this question push him away? If he decides to go through with this, does it mean he is in it with me for the long haul? Or will he only be in it because he feels loyal to our kids but not to me?*

I don't know. I can't know. I don't even think he knows.

The night is a sleepless one for me, even though I am exhausted, spent. There are stormy seas in my dreams. I am on a great big ship, in distress. I am a small speck blindly finding my way through. Family, friends, known entities are there somewhere, but they are dark shadows in gray fog. I can't make out any faces in the turmoil.

I wake to my thoughts on repeat: *What to do? What to do? What to do?!?* I am seeking. Seeking and finding nothing.

What I do know is that I love Mark. Much of our lives overlap in what sparks joy for us—how we interact with our friends, family, and the world. I think I would like to share this with him, would be grateful for his participation in this way, but I don't want to rush him or force his hand. It's enough that I'm having to rush myself.

As the waves of information and feelings continue to collide in me, I am at a loss of how to sift through them. I truly want to hide away. Not from cancer, but from the future decisions cancer is forcing upon me and those around me. I just want to focus on the moment, but my life is no longer only about me and the moment.

Even though we don't know what choices our future selves will need, Mark and I separately get dressed, brush our teeth, and meet up to attend the follow-up fertility appointment together the next morning. We have somehow bucked ourselves up to be ready— ready to sign documents, ready to show up for this next step.

This, in and of itself, is something. Though it is a small step, the forward motion is reliable, reassuring—something from the us before that is sticking in this new territory.

I, of course, had to cancel my flight for South Africa, but Mark tells me this morning that he canceled his too—so he could stay and be here for me. A part of me yearns to hold onto this action tightly. *Maybe it means he sees a future together*, I think.

"Please don't read too much into this," he says, anticipating my thoughts.

I try not to, even though hearing this request makes me want to cry.

"My being here, to contribute, is an insurance policy," Mark says with a small smile, a plea—to himself, to me?—as he squeezes my hand. "Let's not overthink it."

A nurse takes us back to a cramped room and hands me a folder. She pulls out the paperwork, going through our options first.

Gosh, it is hard. Hard, hard, hard. I want to feel relief in Mark's willingness to be here for me, but that is not available to me right now. I'm unable to compartmentalize like he can, and forms must be signed.

"If you create embryos, I need you to decide now who will keep them if you break up," the nurse says.

Fuckin' a. I did not see that coming.

"Lindsay, of course," Mark replies.

Thanks? I want to offer, out loud, but I'm not sure I can be audibly grateful.

I decide then that, in order to be okay with this, I must set aside what these ramifications could mean for now. This is about me getting through this, and that is where I have to keep my attention.

I nod and initial the paperwork, willing my eyes not to swell and myself not to think about the potential pain this paper holds.

I am relieved when the nurse takes the signed document away and replaces it with a calendar indicating which of five different medications—two pills and three injections—to take when. She hands me a large, clear plastic bag of mini jars, compact boxes, and tiny needles in plastic casings and then shows me how to give myself the different injections and in what order. One requires a draw from a vial, one is preloaded and pen-like—where, with a click, medicine is distributed—and one is special, for right before the retrieval, and must be kept refrigerated.

I furiously write notes on the calendar even though she tells me I can watch how-to videos later on YouTube. I don't want to watch how-to videos on YouTube.

And then, right then and there, she has me pinch the skin below my navel to do a practice jab into my abdomen. It feels like a fire drill. The needle is tiny, but a prickle of blood remains when I release the syringe.

I am handed a red sharps container to dispose of the used needles.

"What do I do with this when I'm done?" I ask, giving the vessel a shake.

"You bring it back here and we'll take care of it, or take it to a pharmacy," the nurse tells me. She speaks quickly, having other patients to get to, having squeezed me in to accommodate my timeline.

She is used to cancer requiring immediacy, interrupting a regular day. I, on the other hand, am not. I feel unprepared, and she can sense it.

"Do you have all that?" she asks, stopping, looking at my notes.

"I guess so," I say, not ready to lift myself out of the chair.

The infertility doctor pops his head in and gives me his cell phone number—to reach out if anything comes up. This is unexpectedly comforting because something *might* come up. How should I know? This is cancer we're dealing with, not normal circumstances.

4 | spilling out

When my mom arrives, she and our friend Mila, also South African, attend the next back-to-back appointments with me.

Mila is very special to me. She and my mom were introduced through a mutual friend when we all lived in Texas—she in Houston, our family in Dallas—before we moved to Colorado. They struck up an instant friendship, as my mom has felt a kinship to Africa for as long as I can recall and, in Mila, she found an entity embodying that deep, overlapping affection for a place. They kept in touch for maybe twenty years before she became *my* friend, too, for a different kind of overlap.

Mila is the reason I met Mark.

Before I moved from Los Angeles to San Francisco, I scouted out some apartments in SF one Labor Day weekend. On the sunny last day before my five-hour drive south back to LA, Mila agreed to an obligatory "can you meet my daughter?" cappuccino. We instantly giggled like long-lost friends despite our decades of age difference; something about starting fresh somewhere reverberated between us. We couldn't wait till we met again.

And the next time happened to be at a café near my new home, where she would introduce me to her South African nephew's wife, Anel, who had also recently relocated to SF with her husband. We, too, became fast friends.

A year into my San Francisco life, Anel had a birthday party and invited all her South African friends that she and her husband had met through a South African business club. I attended with my boyfriend at the time, a talented filmmaker and animator, who I was on the fritz with because of fundamental differences in our life beliefs (he was a serious Christian and I was not).

We were seated at one end of the table when Mark walked into the restaurant with a female friend—to join the party at the other end of the table. I recall this moment as if he were backlit and illuminated, looking like Patrick Dempsey as McDreamy from *Grey's Anatomy*. I instantly felt like I knew him even though I knew nothing about him.

I was also jealous. Jealous of the girl he entered with—that she was the recipient of his laughter and attention and I was not.

A couple of months later, after my old boyfriend and I had parted ways, I ran into one of Mark's roommates, who I had met at the party, on the bus home from work; soon after, I saw another of his roommates at a rooftop party to watch the Blue Angels with Anel. Things were brewing behind the scenes. Sharing of Facebook profiles. Talks of all doing something sometime.

And then one Saturday morning at The Grove on Fillmore, a cozy and casual dining spot a couple of blocks down from my apartment (and a few blocks across from Mark's apartment), Mila, Anel, and I ran into Mark and his roommates. Anel introduced them all to Mila, we left them to eat their breakfast in peace, and then after a few giggly steps down the road, she quickly turned around to invite them all to dinner that evening at Mila's home in Belvedere.

They said yes.

This was the beginning of our courtship.

And I say "courtship" because it took Mark a few months and a few friend-filled get-togethers to give me a peck on the lips goodnight and ask me out, just us.

He was never one to make decisions swiftly, and here life was, speeding up the process.

The night before we were supposed to travel to South Africa, Mark, my mom, and I go out for dinner. We're back at The Grove, for its ease, convenience, and comfort. It is already dark outside and the fairy lights on the trees lining Fillmore Street are visible through the café windows. Mila had already said her goodbyes for the day.

I don't know yet if Mark will fertilize any eggs to create embryos, but he seems probably 85 percent there, leaning into it, to give me—and possibly, us—the potential for a future child. Maybe even children.

We grab the only available spot to sit down, a table near where others line up to place their orders. We all scoot in close over the glossy wood surface between us to hear each other. The pendant light above creates a halo around Mark's chestnut curls.

We fill Mark in on the day, namely, how the breast surgeon deemed herself "the local sheriff" and the oncologist "the FBI." The surgeon said it was her job to take out the lump and test the margins—the rim of tissue surrounding the tumor—to see if there was any localized spread of the cancer; the oncologist would then use a CT scan and MRI to see if there was any "all-over" spread—cancer in other areas of my body. The oncologist, soft-spoken and patient, thankfully didn't list all the possible complications or worries.

I also tell Mark that two things got cleared up: the breast

surgeon said my lumpectomy will coincide with my egg retrieval mid-December and to not worry about the timing (I used that handy cell number my IVF doc gave me to call him and confirm); and the oncologist said I *will* have to undergo chemotherapy because my cancer is rapidly dividing, as per the pathology results of my biopsy. He'll need it to tackle any micro spread that the scans can't pick up. I'll begin in January.

My mom leans in and asks Mark how he is doing.

It's a lot of information to take in at once, but his focus is on the significance of the day. Of the trip we are missing.

"I was just really looking forward to taking Lindsay to our family's house on the river in the Eastern Cape," he says, and his breath catches.

Oh my, I flinch. *He is about to cry.*

He chokes out, "I miss it there," and a quiet sob escapes as my mom reaches out to him across the table.

I watch, stunned by the release of his feelings but also by the distance I feel from them, having already let go of our trip, not realizing he was still holding on. And anyway, my mind keeps sliding elsewhere, to my upcoming checklist: CT scan tomorrow, then an MRI, a mammogram, and I can't forget the injections… I am unable to be present.

"Are you scared?" my mom asks, redirecting her attention from Mark to me so he can pull himself together away from her gaze.

Her worried expression searches mine, presumably dreading the chasm still to cross, not sure what to do with anyone's feelings, her own threatening to spill out in the background (which they do at my apartment after dinner, and again, I can't help them, can't solve them, can't pick them up or patch them. I am still so far away in my mind, down the road of to-do's).

"The not-knowing was the worst!" I say, feeling this truth release in me. The diagnosis felt dreadful, but moving forward does not. "I'm not saying these next steps are going to be easy, but I just know that I will get through it."

No one gave me a prognosis in terms of life or death, so I'm not seeing this as life or death. Even though the nurse who gave me all the possible outcomes of what my diagnosis could entail was *the worst*, in a way, she prepared me. By getting the most shocking possibilities out on the table first, I am now able to appreciate the relatively neutral experience of getting to my prescribed course of action.

But my declaration doesn't take anyone else's worry away.

5 | vague shapes

Imogen, these first few weeks, I don't have a lot of humor at the ready. I have my head down, focused—making sure I don't miss a step. As I get to the end of my injections, I feel like a mother hen carrying around an exorbitant number of eggs with a waddling gait and an inner worry not to torque any of the ligaments holding them in place.

Mark and I decide to move forward with him fertilizing some of my eggs. That requires reviewing additional legalese about what we would do if we had embryos we wouldn't use: release them to science or discard them. It isn't fun and it isn't easy to come up with our answer. I want to lean into science, but this makes Mark nervous, thinking a potential child of ours could be used for who-even-knows-what, so we agree to discard them.

We also both have to have a psych evaluation by a middle-aged woman who very much feels combative and not on our side. "If you don't know, you *shouldn't* do it," she emphasizes to each of us, separately.

I really wish I didn't have to sit through her interrogation, but I do. I make things up with as much sincerity as I can summon so we can just get on with it and she can give her "stamp of approval." I mean, who made her God?

The MRI is the most disturbing for me, though—having my boobs dangling through two circular holes while lying still, shirtless, in a confined tube for nearly forty-five minutes. I have an IV poking into my arm at an uncomfortable angle and a construction-like pounding penetrating my skull.

No way do I want to repeat that experience! I tell myself, nearly running out of the hospital when I finish to gasp in the cold winter air and expose my face to some vitamin D.

My oncologist and I meet again to review the results. Thankfully, no visible spread of cancer appeared on either the CT scan or MRI.

"Any family history of breast cancer?" he asks, leaning against the countertop behind him with his arms casually crossed over his waist. My shoulders relax at his straightforward line of questioning, for this moment of normalcy—me sitting fully clothed across from him, knowing nothing else is lurking in those diagnostic images.

"Yes, my paternal grandmother had breast cancer," I say.

"At what age?"

"She was in her seventies."

"Oh, so postmenopausal," he notes and picks up his clipboard.

"Yes, I guess so." *Hmm, does this matter?* I wonder, hearing the scratch of his ballpoint pen as it underlines this detail.

"Do you have Jewish lineage in your family?"

"I do—on my dad's side."

His eyes follow the clipboard as he sets it down on the counter, then look back up to mine.

"Well, I'd like you to have a blood test to see if you are a carrier of the BRACK-uh gene, spelled B-R-C-A. It could explain why you have cancer at such a young age."

This is the first I hear of BRCA. This is years before Angelina Jolie tells the world that she has BRCA1 in an op-ed for *The New York Times*.

"What does BRCA have to do with being Jewish?" An instinctual defensiveness arises in me. I want to know.

"The BRCA gene appears more frequently in individuals with an Ashkenazi Jewish background than the general population."

I audibly blow out some air, given I do happen to know my paternal grandparents are of Ashkenazi descent.

I often pride myself on being the one kid of my father's who actually paid attention in Sunday School. I learned Hebrew and was able to recite the prayers with a friend, singing a cappella in the snow one night walking back from class in Boulder, despite opting out of a bat mitzvah. But in this moment in my oncologist's office, coming face-to-face with my heritage, I mostly recall the hurt: visiting the Holocaust Museum in Washington, DC, and seeing the hundreds of shoes, from heels and boots to tiny baby shoes, piled up, and then a few years later, seeing the charred hollows of Dachau's crematoriums on a visit in high school. On some cellular level, these horrors had always pertained to me.

But now I feel again the familiar guilt that comes with choosing to be Jew-*ish*, nonpracticing, like when I ate leavened bread or enjoyed a margarita the week of Passover, as my LA roommate pointed out to me. Because now I'm wondering, what part of being Jewish is a choice? There is far more to it than religious customs, cultural rituals, and collective trauma.

"Let's just have you do a test and *then* we can discuss more of what it could mean, going forward," my oncologist remarks, "if it is positive."

Even though I thought the biggest worries were behind us, I

do love how matter-of-fact and piecemeal he is with his information. Could he sense the storm in me brewing?

"Okay," I say.

Imogen, it isn't until my lumpectomy—two days before my egg retrieval—that I realize I feel completely disconnected to the actual cancer in my body.

I'm not angry at it or resentful and really have no finger on any palpable pulse of energy associated with it. The energy, strangely, is more around the word *cancer* itself and the chain of events my diagnosis set off.

Nonetheless, just as quickly as the cancer appeared, I am ready for it to disappear.

The outpatient clinic for the removal of my two-centimeter lump is small and quiet. No one else is in the waiting room when my mom and I arrive, but we whisper anyway.

We sit beside each other as I flip through the pre-surgery forms, writing in my details and passively signing where required, a drill I've quickly become familiar with: HIPAA (privacy) rights, insurance details, a list of my current medications and doctors. For those, I am prepared.

But when I come to the last page and read *in case of death* and *if you remain unconscious*, I stop myself. *Sheesh*, I think. I didn't anticipate *these* questions.

I lean over to show my mom.

"Oh, it's a medical affidavit, sweetie," she quickly responds, giving the page a once-over. "Just protocol when undergoing general anesthesia. This is common, boilerplate stuff. Don't worry about it."

But I do worry about it. This is the first time I've ever had to literally sign my life away. I scribble in her name and my dad's for who to make decisions for me shall I remain unconscious. I wonder if I should write in Mark's name, too, when it hits me that I am actually having something cut out of my body and that Mark doesn't really know my parents and what would there really be for them to discuss if I died on the table?

I breathe. My mom just sits there and rubs my back as I get through the rest of the page.

"I guess I haven't had a surgery before, unless you count having my wisdom teeth removed," I say, deciding not to voice that I didn't actually think about dying until now. Knowing my mom's motto of "If it's meant to be, it will be," I'm not interested in discussing the possibility of my dying on the table being meant to be.

So, I settle myself. *There is no turning back now, Lindsay,* I say internally. *The river is already moving.*

My insides still in response. I know I am in good hands.

It is soon time to leave my contacts and glasses behind in a locker, along with my clothes. When I'm in a gown and flat on my back, being wheeled down the hall to the operating room, I only see vague shapes of the overhead lights and shadows on the walls. My breast surgeon's assertive cadence pacifies me, as she reiterates the procedure she will perform.

There are more bodies in the room than I thought there would be—helping, assisting, monitoring. Since I can't make out their faces and don't have to determine who they are, I let their background movement soothe me.

The surgeon calls a day later to confirm that the cancer has not spread to my lymph nodes and that my margins are clear. This should land as hugely relieving, but it just feels like one less thing to think about as I give myself my final injection—a "trigger shot"—to finalize the maturation of my eggs for Saturday's retrieval.

My parents tag-team. My mom returns to Colorado, and my dad arrives for the weekend.

We all show up at the IVF clinic—me, Mark, and my dad—to meet the infertility doc. The day is bright and crisp, like when I first got the call in my office two weeks earlier, and the elevators at the end of a long, empty hallway take us up to the retrieval floor.

At some point, between the numerous 7:00 a.m. appointments to monitor my hormone levels and follicle growth, I'd told my doc that my dad shares his profession. When the elevator doors open, my doc is there to receive us, like a host welcoming us into his own home. Minimal staff are present. He shakes hands with my dad and their easy camaraderie portrays them both in their element.

A nurse leads me back to put on a gown, tuck my belongings into a cubby, and receive an IV for "twilight" anesthesia.

Later, I am told that Mark is called from the waiting area to a private room for his sperm collection, and when he returns a few minutes later, my dad offhandedly comments with his signature loud, throaty laugh, "That was quick. It won't always be so easy."

Thankfully, this garners a laugh in response, and some humor makes it through to us after all.

I wake up to see "23" written on my hand in blue ink.

I am in and out of awareness, sensing my abdomen in one tight cramp. The nurse tells me this is a good outcome—the number—likely because of my age and that I've been on the pill.

How does she know that? I wonder, as my eyes slip back into sleep.

She places a warm water bottle-like compress under the sheet, above my gown, along my midsection. The heat is heavenly and I relax.

Later, when I'm more awake, my doc confirms that of the eggs retrieved, twenty-two are mature.

"How many would you like to fertilize?" he asks. "I suggest fifteen, leaving seven eggs, giving you plenty of options."

Sounds like plenty, Mark and I agree.

The next day, we are informed that six of the fifteen eggs fertilized.

That seems like a much more reasonable amount to store for future options than fifteen potential children, and I feel comfortable receiving this news.

Three days later, I get a call that five embryos remain dividing and are, therefore, viable enough to freeze for a potential transfer at a later date. With five years of storage fees covered as a fertility preservation patient, I am grateful for the freedom to tuck away any childbearing decisions for now.

6 | as many owls as possible

As I come to the end of what feels like a marathon crammed into a sprint, and just before a flight home to join my family in Colorado for the holidays, my dad asks me to go with him for a walk around Alta Plaza Park.

A walk? Sure, I can handle a walk.

The cherry blossoms that usually fill the trees next to the tiered walkways are long absent, but, indicative of Bay Area winters, the hills beside us are lush with long green grass. I look out past Pierce Street to the sun glinting off the Golden Gate Bridge, savoring the details, when I hear, "Do you want to get a second opinion?"

"For what, Dad?" I ask, matching his pace.

"For your care moving forward."

Hmmm, easy question. Easy answer.

"No, I feel good about the doctors I have."

"Well, I think we should get a second opinion when we're back home," he pushes, as gently as possible. "It is the smart thing to do."

I turn toward him and finally register the concern in his questioning. Even though I disagree, I don't have the energy to push back. Maybe because we're outside and the air feels cleansing, or because I've tackled a few scary things already, this doesn't feel so scary—just time-consuming, and I'm tired.

He's probably bringing this up because *he* needs a second opinion for his own sense of security in a place he knows and trusts. He wasn't at those first appointments with me. My brain has a smidgen of space now to realize this.

"Okay," I concede.

Mark stops by that afternoon with a gift for me.

"Merry Christmas," he says.

I carefully unwrap the small, heavy items nestled in tissue paper to find two identical painted owl figures. It doesn't take me long to recognize that they are an exact match to the one he gave me as a gift last year.

"To watch over you while you're away," he tells me, mirroring the sentiment of the first one that now resides on my desk.

"Oh, thank you," I say, holding them, wondering why I need two more.

Maybe this sort of situation requires as many owls as possible, I chuckle internally, noting that this wasn't what I was expecting before we went our separate ways for the holidays. Nonetheless, I stow both into my suitcase, appreciating his thoughtfulness.

My dad gets me an appointment with a renowned medical oncologist at the University of Colorado. We see her the day after we fly in. I'm not too pleased to—again—hear the hard truths of my diagnosis, to share them with another stranger, or succumb to another breast exam. But, because I love my dad and tend to give him more leeway in the compassion department, I endure it.

I feel especially relieved—and validated—when the doctor gives me the exact same protocol, to a T, as the San Francisco specialists for how to move forward.

Now we can stop thinking about that! I nod to myself on our way out.

But on the drive home, my dad surprises me with a question that isn't on my radar—not even a little bit.

"Do you want to do your treatments here, honey?" he asks once we're out of Denver and closer to the prairies that slope up against the base of Pikes Peak. "Your mom and I would really love to have you."

I can feel the parental need and worry beneath the surface, and I don't want to hurt his feelings. But I also know I can't do it.

"No. Thanks though, Dad," I say and peek over at him. He seems okay, so I continue, "I really want to stay in San Francisco. I love it there, and I feel good about my doctors and my setup."

I don't want to whine, but a part of me is gearing up to if he pushes back. Not only do I not want to revert back to being cooped up under their watchful eye, but I don't want to be away from the city and friends I've come to feel the most *me* around. And what's more, I want to remain in control of my care. Be my own driver. This dignity is important to me.

I am thankful when he says, "Okay, sweetie" and doesn't fight me on this decision.

When we return to my mom and sister that afternoon, I place one of Mark's owls at the base of a pine tree overlooking my parent's home, thinking, *to watch over them all in my absence.*

It's not until January that I start to wonder why the cancer appeared. Once I am back in my apartment in San Francisco with a couple of cozy new sweaters, an album of peaceful images of the snow on my phone, and some purple and blond streaks in my hair from a salon that my sister and I visited in the spirit of having a little fun before it all falls out, the words that some old high school friends said to me over the break whirl around in my head:

Oh, this couldn't have happened to a better person!

But you are so young and so healthy, I don't get it!

This does not make any sense!

Well, I am quite stressed at work, I think as I recount how many days I fill with longer hours, takeout for lunch, and microwaveable meals for dinner. *Could those things have contributed to this sudden onset?*

Other words add to the whirl, like the ones from Eckhart Tolle that are taped to my bedroom door:

Why are you having this experience? Because this is the experience you need.

This too shall pass.

But those surface Band-Aids only provide momentary relief for the time it takes me to read them.

I am eager for more.

A friend gives me a book called *Love, Medicine and Miracles* by Bernie Siegel, MD, and in it I read that how one takes in or internalizes stress—mentally and emotionally—can affect their immunity, which, in turn, can allow cells to not be tended to appropriately by their genetic makeup. This can even happen because one's inner peace is off-kilter.

Sure, perhaps, I think, and pause to reflect. It isn't enough to solve any problems, but it plants a seed, per se—one that I want to keep tending.

And as I tend, I start to notice how my chest tightens every time I worry about the opinions of others. I stop to consider: *Am I holding others' needs before my own?* And, *Why does it feel like I can't breathe when I ask this question?*

Maybe a therapist can help me gain some answers.

I find a practitioner nearby through my insurance. Within a day, I'm sitting in a room inside a small, old, one-story building in the Richmond district—a few neighborhoods closer to the ocean, thicker into the city's cloud cover. The fog pushes up against the windows.

It takes me mere seconds to know I do not connect to this woman *at all*.

Too bad there isn't a quick-release hatch I can pull to escape.

She is young, going through the motions, and keeps trying to make me talk by asking annoying textbook questions that I feel I must make up answers to just to respond. Meaningless words float from my mouth.

She sits like a statue and offers nothing in return.

No compassion, no understanding—not even advice.

She is blank-face McGee already having me dive into my childhood—for what reason? Maybe there is some caretaking to uncover there, but I don't like hearing my own meandering voice, nor do I like being left to my own devices to draw correlations when it is her expertise I'm wanting. We have no rapport.

This is an experience I do not want to repeat, much like the in-house psychologist I was required to sit down with at the IVF clinic before my retrieval: a grueling session during which I felt like a kid in trouble answering her questions with the most conviction I could muster when I was uncertain as hell about Mark sticking around in my future. Yet, she wouldn't let me pass GO until I convinced her otherwise, leaving me out on a figurative limb to comfort myself.

And so, I leave, knowing I will not return.

The results for the BRCA gene test arrive shortly thereafter and I am called in to discuss them. To my surprise, it is with a genetic counselor and not my doctor. *Here we go again.*

From the get-go, she treads very lightly with the information she presents, like I am fragile. This gets my hackles up right away, because I immediately feel distant from anyone expressing feelings of pity toward me. I am adamant not to collect woes, yet they keep coming.

The counselor nervously reads facts from a pamphlet:

"You are a carrier of the BRCA1 genetic mutation. As a BRCA1 carrier, you are more susceptible to having breast cancer than someone who is not a carrier and since you have breast cancer already, you are more likely to develop a second breast cancer than a carrier who hasn't yet had breast cancer." She shows me some graphs, points to a chart, and continues: "You also have a higher risk of ovarian cancer later in life. Men who are carriers have a slightly heightened risk of breast and prostate cancers, but it largely affects females."

Just pile it on! I think, and, oh she does, going on to explain that I could be a candidate for a preventative double mastectomy surgery, but it would mean I wouldn't be able to breastfeed, if I wanted that someday.

How and when I'd like to participate in parenting is so far away from this present reality that I'd like to just get through this barrier between me and the rest of my life already, thank you very much.

Again, someone who is not my doctor is dishing out all these possibilities.

"You could also have your ovaries removed, called an oophorectomy, before menopause as a preventative measure for ovarian cancer. Having BRCA1, your risk is heightened for that as well."

I am rendered mute a second time. I just want to collect the paperwork and go so I can talk to my doctor about my specific case and best path forward. But she, aggravatingly, continues: "This can feel really lonely, but there are others like you!" She plasters on a saccharine smile and hands me another pamphlet. "Here is a club you can join online!"

She describes this online "club" of other young females. Their faces are decaled with hearts on the glossy cardstock she sets in my hand. "You get free admission the first two years, being a cancer patient."

Oh, for fuck's sake.

"And you can become pen pals with other women your age who are going through what you're going through..."

I stand up. I can no longer take it.

"Is that it?" I ask, grabbing my things.

"Yes."

At least she has the decency to read the room.

I am out of there.

I do not need a fact lesson from a young person who has not been in my shoes, nor is a doctor, *and* speaks to me with trepidation. I don't leave it at that, though. I keep overthinking it on my walk home, my thoughts ping-ponging back and forth, shouting at each other:

Was that rude of me?

She was only trying to help, Lindsay!

Yes, but I don't need to think about all this future stuff right now!

Do I want others to talk to?

No, especially not anyone who might be feeling sorry for themselves!

After I calm down, I can understand why hospitals use genetic counselors as go-betweens to make sure their patients get all the facts before they speak to their doctors. Maybe even to save their doctors time. But my whole self just keeps telling me this is something I am passing through. It will not cripple me. It will not define me.

When I next see my oncologist, I start by asking him about all the possible scenarios the genetic counselor set before me. He holds up his hand.

"Let's not go too far into the future yet."

Thank you.

Don't second-guess yourself, Lindsay!

"We'll just take things one step at a time," he says.

I knew I loved this doctor. Such a lighter approach! Not needing to weigh more decisions today, he lets the fact settle in that I, indeed, have the BRCA1 gene.

At home, I throw my coat on my bed, then take the ten steps over to my computer. My desk is in front of a bay window, four flights up from the sidewalk I just stepped in from. I log on to Facebook to check my messages and see a new one from another

South African friend of Mark's that I am just getting to know.

She says she and her husband recently had dinner with Mark and heard what I was going through. She wants to help and would like to refer me to her shaman.

What? Do I need a shaman? I wonder, now sitting down, conjuring up visions of an old man chanting with a stick. I read on that she even called him in advance of this note to see if he's dealt with this kind of thing before.

He says he had a dream about you, so maybe you are meant to go visit! her message reads. *He is a regular guy…his office is in Mill Valley, but it is super relaxing over there. Here is his number…*

I write it down on my desktop calendar.

He is booked up but call him and see if you can work something out.

"Hold on…" I say out loud to the screen. "How did he have a dream about me?"

That is really weird, but a regular guy in a relaxing space could be worth checking out. I read on that he is also a rabbi and a licensed marriage and family therapist.

This feels interesting and my spine straightens like this question inside me is getting bigger and my spirit has cast a wider signal that this shaman somehow picked up on and raised his hand to help.

The BRCA1 gene might explain why I have cancer at such a young age, but I'm still curious why the cancer grew *now*. I pick up the phone to leave my details on his confidential voice mail.

The morning of my first chemotherapy session is quiet and overcast.

Am I nervous? Only a little.

I'm mostly grateful to feel like I'm being looked after so well and that my mom has flown back out to be with me. I even have a smile on my face.

I enjoy a lighthearted conversation about *American Idol* with the phlebotomist as he draws blood to read my white blood cell count levels, making the entire endeavor effortless and easy. Then I step over to a scale and share a friendly exchange with a nurse who logs my weight and blood pressure, while telling me about getting her daughter off to school this morning. When I enter the infusion room, the two chemo-specific nurses are so welcoming and chatty that I am instantly at ease and equally unfazed by the transition.

Is this really what all the fuss is about? I think, setting my things down and taking a seat. *It's not so bad.*

More chitter-chatter ensues, much like when I am in front of the mirror at the hairdresser's, as the female nurse extends my arm and ties a tourniquet to prep me for my IV.

I look around at the other patients. Everyone is subdued and quiet. Some are sleeping or staying warm, wrapped up in blankets. Some have a friend or family member sitting near them. I think of how I'm not only here with my mom, but with my friends, too—in spirit—from their support that got me here: one who introduced me to her acupuncturist that I'll see later in the week to help combat nausea and strengthen my "chi," another who printed the notes she so meticulously took during a previous appointment, now a handy highlighted reference on my bedside table of what side effects to expect when, and others who have sent meals, baked goods, and well wishes.

The nurse gives me a saline flush intravenously first.

Weird I can taste that, I think as the flavor of salt brightens in the back of my mouth, mixing with my saliva.

A bag of Kool-Aid-red liquid is attached next on a slow drip: the drugs, Adriamycin and Cyclophosphamide (AC).

"This will take about forty-five minutes to an hour," the nurse tells me and my mom, who is sitting in a spare recliner next to me, before she leaves us to check on another patient.

Seeing as nothing is hurting or instantly bothering me, I gaze out the window and see Sutro Tower above Twin Peaks, and then the dentistry school across the street. I don't feel anything except the cool liquid entering my veins. My mom pulls out her book to read, so I reach down into my canvas tote to do the same.

Once the plastic pouch of AC empties, my IV is removed and a dressing is placed over the injection site. My mom collects our bags and coats to wait for me in the lobby while the infusion nurse leads me into an adjacent exam room. She has me expose the skin on my hip for my first Lupron shot.

"You'll have these once a month during chemo," she clarifies.

Over time, the Lupron will put me in a chemical menopause, and

I'll feel a few hot flashes, finally understanding the sensation my grandmother would declare herself having—with exasperation!—when I'd visit her. I do find them quite exasperating but more comical and startling than detrimental in their random and short-lived appearances.

I later see on my medical bills that this one shot costs thousands of dollars. That, in addition to seeing the tens (and sometimes hundreds) of thousands each infusion costs, have me nearly in tears—overwhelmed in gratitude for the COBRA insurance coverage I have from work and the workman's comp I'm receiving.

These were both things that the volunteer, Carol, insisted I fill out paperwork for, to have signed by a supervisor. I initially balked, not understanding that the financial stress of this regimen alone could be enough to kill anyone.

Each time an envelope hosting an Explanation of Benefits reaches me, I read through it with equal parts horror and relief.

The next week, I have my first appointment with the shaman.

I don't know what to expect when I arrive at his building in Mill Valley and approach timidly. I find my way to his office—up an outdoor stairwell, along a narrow balcony, through a propped-open exterior door into a short hallway.

I take a seat on the chair closest to the entry. On the wall in front of me is a Zen painting of a small house tucked into a mountainside. On the table beside me, I notice a few small stones, a feather, and a bumpy shell in a formation, purposefully placed.

A good ten minutes pass before the door to the shaman's office opens and his previous client, a middle-aged man, leaves. I smile as he walks past me, hoping to silently detect something about the experience from his expression, but he offers no eye contact, making a quick exit.

I then stand up to meet the shaman with a quiet hello, lifting my hand in a wave. He isn't an old, skinny man with a long, white beard, nor is he covered in feathers or animal skins. He is of average height and weight, with a wide smile that makes the corners of his eyes crinkle. He exudes warmth and jolliness beneath the casual business attire of a sweater and pants.

He bows his head, which is covered in tight salt-and-pepper curls, and I am immediately struck with a feeling of familiarity and fellowship.

In his doorway, he offers me some brown rice tea, which I accept—*something to do and focus on,* I think. I notice a tiny kitchen with an electric kettle and some mugs in a closet off the hallway behind him. He invites me to find a seat in his room while he makes the tea.

Inside, there are a few potted plants, low-lit lamps, and the smell of sage wafts in the air. I find my way over to one of the two brown leather loveseats beside a large picture window that frames a grove of redwood trees outside.

The shaman enters, extends a handleless ceramic cup of steaming liquid to me, then sits cross-legged in a matching chair facing my seat, angled at the corner of a large kilim rug.

The tea is hot. I set it down on the side table, next to a box of tissues that I hope I don't need.

"I'm just going to check in first, okay?" the shaman says. He nods, as if answering his own question, then closes his eyes.

His forefinger and thumb rub a powdery substance in a small dish on the table next to him and he takes an audible inhale. "*Pfu…*" he breathes and blows out his breath with a look of distaste on his pursed mouth, then inhales again.

Uh oh, what is so gross to him? I wonder, trying to read his expression. But I sit still, my eyes wide and brow furrowed.

This continues for a couple of minutes and then he opens his eyes to speak. He is lively again and present.

"I was clearing you," he explains. "Tasting the toxicity of the medicine in your body."

Hearing that makes me want to recoil, but seeing that he is okay, I instead say, "Thank you?"

He is quiet again. We spoke over the phone, but I take this opportunity to reiterate my question about why this cancer appeared in my body *now* and if it could be from holding other people's "stuff" in my chest.

He then tells me about the "upper world," "middle world" (where we exist now), and the "lower world."

Oh, gosh, I like that distinction, I think, and tell him about a dream I had recently where I felt a ghost-like soul overtake my body and I wrestled to shove it out.

"That is the lower world," he says. "I want you to practice grounding yourself here in the middle world, to protect yourself from the energies of others—and to bring *your* energy back into you."

He stands up to show me a stance of what groundedness looks like: knees bent, feet firmly planted on the floor.

"Feel into the solid surface supporting you," he says.

I get up and mirror his pose.

He explains that I am projecting most of my energy outside of myself.

We work on how I can retain my energy by grounding myself, replenishing my energy from the "upper," and shifting what I offer others to be more like 30 percent outside myself, keeping 70 percent inside.

I nod.

This framework is almost overwhelmingly simple, yet a hugely clear distinction for me to grasp. I feel like we're getting somewhere. That me showing up here today is helping.

We sit back down.

He then tells me the upper world wants to be let in, to love me unconditionally; it wants to pour in light and hold me in comfort as if I am a baby cradled in its arms.

Mmm, that sounds nice, I think and try to envision myself in the light of the upper world's arms. But it is hard to fully wrap my mind around. I can feel a part of me is shut off, inaccessible.

He checks in again, breathing with his eyes closed. I sit silently breathing as well.

He opens his eyes momentarily to tell me, "I'm just going to bring in some of the upper world now," then closes them again.

As he breathes, I kid you not, a glowing yellow light emanates from him, outlining all the objects in the room, and my eyes fill with tears. I blink a few times wondering if my sight is playing a trick on me, but the light holds, the glow amplifies, and my chest expands.

As I sit there breathing, I feel a subtle vibration within me as if a volume knob is being turned up on my spirit self.

I grab for the box of tissues. *Dang it*, I think as I sniff, not wanting to be seen as anything but strong, yet unable to stop.

The walls I didn't even know I was holding up crumble.

"That is your grief," the shaman tells me when he opens his eyes again. "It is okay to let the upper world hold it for you."

By session two of chemo, I am more lethargic. My hair is still mostly there, coming out in loose strands in the shower but no alarmingly large clumps.

My brother visits for the weekend and we have a head-shaving party. Mark brings the clippers. I tell myself I'm on the offense, controlling my hair loss before it can control me.

But I am sad. There is still loss here and I'm feeling it. The loss of what I thought I'd be doing otherwise; the loss of something normal. Those expectations fall to the floor with my hair, to the upper world.

I cover my head with a loosely knitted white beanie, which I'll select the most in the coming months. I have two wigs, too, that I picked up with my mom on her last visit (also at Carol's insistence). I didn't want them. It felt indulgent to have them for such a short period of time and indicative of something I still really don't want to be associated with, but they end up as the best disguises for social situations when I want to blend in.

It takes until my third chemo infusion to be completely bald.

My scalp has freckles I've, understandably, never seen before. All the other hair on my body also disappears—on my arms, my eyebrows, my eyelashes. The weirdest part for me is the hair I didn't even realize was there—faintly covering my face—that, when missing, makes my skin feel baby-like each time I sweep my knuckles across the side of my cheek.

I ask Mark how it is, seeing me completely hairless on the pillow beside him. He assures me I am still beautiful—hair or no hair.

Seeing as each time I pass a mirror, I need to remind my startled brain that the person I glimpse is me, I am unable to believe him.

Before I know it, I am even more fatigued after treatments.

So much so that any emotions I have indelibly turn to tears. Especially around Mark.

Why isn't he bending over backward tending to my every need and declaring his never-ending love for me in the face of all this change?

I keep hoping he'll whisk me through this phase with some romantic distraction. But I also have this double standard that I don't want to be treated any differently. And this is where he shows up. And keeps showing up.

So much has changed, keeps changing, and it's like he has

blinders on and won't look at me any differently. Mark doesn't coddle me, nor bend unnaturally toward me in a way that is uncomfortable for him. He has no magic key to get me out of this moment or through it any faster.

But could I use a safe embrace to sink into?

Yes, yes, I could.

When my emotions rise high and I air my frustrations in how his actions aren't syncing up with what I think they should be, we have proper fights.

When my drained energy miraculously passes after a day or two of rest, I feel much stronger.

I come around to appreciating that Mark is still present, listening, and has an ability to sit in the tornado of my feelings and be unshakable.

This helps me to remember it is my turn to tend to my needs. Not his.

Acupuncture appointments continue to be a welcome antidote to my infusions, where I have that built-in someone beckoning me into their space for rest. The pinprick and twist of the needle is never particularly enjoyable—especially between my toes or at the crown of my head—but my brain focuses on their purposes: the cleansing and strengthening properties they provide me.

With my increased exhaustion, it is a pleasure not to have to drive myself to these appointments. One weekday morning, the founder of the company I work for, who we call Martinez, shows up outside my apartment complex in his zippy green Mini Cooper, ready for the task.

I remember disbelieving this moment—how he, like Jan, goes out of his way to lend a hand. As the forefront of the company, he is always on the go—building business relationships with clients, appearing at different shoots—and not often in the office. Yet here he is, being supremely present and genuinely curious to hear how I am doing and how things are going.

Having cancer is an anomaly to me in this way: an equalizer of sorts, to the most human and caring parts of you. To my young, mid-twenties self, this is a real *namaste* moment (I honor the light in you, and you honor the light in me) where our titles and my position on the career totem pole truly have no relevance.

Only four years earlier, when I first started working in film production as an intern, I'd cold-called Martinez in San Francisco after reading in *The Denver Post* about the production company he'd just started. He was amicable and said he'd meet me for coffee if I was ever in the area, but he currently had the staff he needed.

After my two-year detour to Los Angeles, I showed up again for a, now advertised, role at Martinez's company and got my foot in the door.

Today, two years after that, here we are—perhaps fulfilling an agreement we'd made in an alternate reality to share this very human moment on both of our journeys in life.

It's funny, looking backward, how I remember being more stressed with work than I let on. How, even before all of this cancer business, I paid for a career counselor to give me a lengthy test that would determine where I'd have the most satisfaction work-wise. Spoiler alert: Film production wasn't it.

When I wanted to quit, I had a "boozy" lunch with Martinez, enjoying *one* glass of wine, and the alcohol acted as a truth serum that allowed all my frustrations to release out of me. My tangled gripes rolled right off Martinez's back, but he listened, acknowledging those feelings, and offered a few appealing solutions to my "problems."

After that, I felt validated and *valuable*. I dove back into work with a raise and an enthusiastic "okay, I'll give it another go!" attitude—only to find myself crunched up against situations that weren't making my heart soar.

Perhaps, as the career counselor's test indicated, interior

design was a better way to channel my creative energies—something structured and artistic, that could make a tangible difference in the lives of the individuals living and breathing in the spaces I had a hand in making.

I applied to a master's program where I could learn just that. I was accepted and slated to start after the winter holidays, but once cancer came along, I was able to push out my entrance until fall, staying within my current company's employ during recovery.

What a gift.

I had nothing to do but rest and finally answer that demand I had multiple times earlier to "take a break from all the 'should' do's and 'must' do's" I kept internalizing for work.

It was this diagnosis that forced me to stop, evaluate, pay attention.

There is a Native American saying that—if we use the shaman's terminology—alludes to the "upper world." That, if the upper world wants to send you a message, it first comes in the form of a feather (I'm paraphrasing here)—something subtle. If you don't listen to the brush of the feather, the upper world will then send a message by brick—something harder, more substantial. And, if that goes unnoticed, the message will appear in the form of a rock, or major crisis that literally forces change.

Well, that wish inside me to take a break, try something different, didn't stop me. Trying to quit didn't get me there, either—so here I was, forced into literal change.

What did this change mean? I was still curious, still unable to unveil an obvious "ah-ha!" except to be in the moment, to soak in not needing to be anywhere but here, nor tending to anyone's needs other than my own.

Whatever else life had in store would reveal itself.

I lie down and nap. I read. I blog a little to share my experience with my friends and family still in the daily grind, following along from their desktops near and far. I am quick to take my prescribed pills to prevent nausea. I sip kombucha. Mark also has me squeezing lemon into a mug with hot water to drink each morning as a detox—and drops a handful of lemons by every few days.

I'm not drinking alcohol—because why tax my body when it is already taxed to the max? I'm also not having caffeine. I adopt some of the rules listed by an email forward I keep receiving from friends—of what to do to avoid cancer. I give up dairy, throw out my microwave (literally heaving it down to the curb with a "Free" sign), and try to remember to take ten deep breaths each day as the "most cleansing thing I can do."

The most cleansing thing, I find, is the hardest. Even in the stillness and quiet of space, deep breathing escapes me. Meditation is hard to come by. I let my mind wander. My eyes land on the cherry blossoms now blooming in Alta Plaza Park outside my bay window. I soak up the birds-eye view of the world's busyness below.

Much like my time with the shaman, my connection to the "upper" is being recalled.

All facets of me are present. *I* am in waiting—listening. Being.

Learn to be your own best friend, Lindsay. No one else knows the best answers for you but you, are the messages that appear.

10 | do I really need breasts

Near the end of chemo, I am given a fork in the road: either go through radiation and annual MRIs to check for future breast cancers, or have my breast tissue cut out. I'd rather abstain from the choice, but that's what the BRCA1 gene does: forces one's hand.

Recalling the data from the genetic counselor, I ask my oncologist, "What about the possibility of ovarian cancer?"

"I'll be ordering annual pelvic ultrasounds and CA-125 blood draws for you," he says, "to screen for ovarian cancer."

"But do I need to have my ovaries removed at some point?"

"That is something we can discuss further down the road—when you're forty or forty-five, the age our studies show that you are more at risk."

In the absence of any words from me, my oncologist writes down the name of a radiologist.

"His wife is a patient of mine," he says.

Gulp, that can't be good.

"He can give you more information."

I wonder, with either of these paths, how I can hold onto what I already know of my body or how much more I'll lose along the way.

I talk to the radiologist, the shaman, and my breast surgeon to help me through to the other side of this decision.

The radiologist is exceedingly gentle and approachable, assuring me that I will not put my future in jeopardy by opting out of radiology, should I go the mastectomy route. He has a compassion and understanding about him that comes from firsthand experience. He tells me, too, that if I do radiation and *then* choose to have a mastectomy in the future, the skin at the radiation site will be taut and less pliable, not giving me the cosmetic outcome of a natural-looking breast.

That does it for me, Imogen. I can only see challenges and complications to come if I keep my breast tissue. It is a quick, easy appointment and my path toward a double mastectomy becomes more of a positive one.

But I still feel a lot of stress rooted in removing both of my breasts prophylactically—and then debate whether it is important for me to have reconstruction at all—or if the idea of being left with two scars across my chest feels better (using a padded bra to fill out a shirt or a dress if desired).

I set up an appointment with the shaman to see if he can tap into the "upper world" and reveal what I should do. He is able to sit with me in my discomfort but cannot, nor will not, tell me which choice to make. Ultimately, he offers the guidance to release that which I am unable to figure out to the upper world so that the answer I need can appear.

My breast surgeon gives me the logistics: that I can schedule a double mastectomy with her for July, when it'll be two months post-chemotherapy—the earliest my body can handle with the least amount of time to develop another cancer. July feels rather soon, but also gives me some time to mentally prepare if I proceed with reconstruction.

She tells me the recovery will be at least four to six weeks, possibly longer if I undergo reconstruction. It is here I relay my hesitation.

"Yeah, about that. I mean, do I really need breasts?" I ask.

Again, this isn't her decision and she can't answer this question for me. Instead, she lists the multiple routes I can go these days with different implants or fat harvesting on my own body (*eeish!* I shiver) and hands me a printed roster of plastic surgeons she partners with at the hospital.

"Reach out and schedule a consultation," she directs me, sliding the paper over to me. When I don't immediately grab it, she pulls it back to her side and circles her top two recommendations from the list: one woman and one man.

I meet with the woman first, assuming that she'll just get it. That it'll be easier for me to discuss breasts and the look of breasts with her. A quick Google search beforehand populates a lot of press and accolades: voted *by the people* and *best of* for 2009. She is pretty, put-together, and welcomes the spotlight. The more I absorb, the higher my hopes get that the *joie de vivre* she seemingly has for her profession will ease me over the decision threshold into reconstruction.

Mila accompanies me to the appointment. The doctor, wearing a skirt suit and what I've come to recognize as her signature smile, welcomes us in and closes the door. As we are finding our seats in her office, she pulls a pamphlet out of her desk drawer and hands it to me. It is for Latisse, a prescription medicine for eyelash growth.

"This is so great," she says. "You'll love it. I'll write a script for you now."

"But I'm still undergoing chemotherapy," I say, stunned.

"My eyelashes will grow back."

When she doesn't hear me or respond, I fume. *This is temporary and comes with the treatment,* I argue in my head. *And how did we get here already anyway?*

She shifts gears and launches into her sales pitch.

"We can use saline or silicone implants. Or! Even fatty tissue from your inner thigh…" She grins, then stops to contemplate what she just said as her eyes look me up and down. "That is a more invasive procedure with a longer recovery, and I'll have to take a closer look at you before I can determine which cup size we can get from your body…but I encourage you to go larger than your natural size. All of my clients want to go larger—if you're doing this, you might as well go big, right?"

Umm, no thank you! I think, as my initial impression of her plummets. But she doesn't stop to ask what *I* want.

"We use spacers to stretch the skin, and I'll show you how to do the massaging over time to get your body acclimated to the new size." She takes a breath, again eyeing my chest, then jumps right back in. "We can go over the muscle or under the muscle. I prefer under because it provides a built-in bra, even though, overall, the procedure is slightly more painful…"

She continues as if on a soap box at a motivational conference. I am not finding any of this motivational. I glance over at Mila. Her deer-in-the-headlights expression conveys we are on the same page.

Why did my breast surgeon circle her name? I wonder, when the door to her office opens and a nurse interrupts.

"Could I speak with you a moment?" she asks the doctor.

I hear wailing in the distance, presumably of a patient in one of the exam rooms.

"Yes, of course!" she tells the nurse, then turns to me. "I'll be right back. Why don't you step into that robe while I'm out?"

My eyes follow her finger to a thick brown garment hanging

on a coat rack next to her desk.

"When I return," she continues, "I can answer my own question about what cup size we could salvage from your inner thigh."

She leaves to, I think, address the patient in tears. Mila and I just stare at each other. That cry is concerning.

"I guess I'll put on the robe?" I say slowly. *Is this her robe? Is this for patients? Is this even clean?* It's hard to tell in the faint lamplight.

"I'll look over here while you get dressed," Mila says.

I grumble to her about the doctor's inappropriate sale of Latisse while changing and complain that I don't want her to pinch my fat and see what she can harvest from my body for something I might not even want.

How did she even win all those awards? I judge as I try to shake off her pushiness.

Once I have the robe on, Mila and I sit quietly in our chairs with our knees crossed. Framed magazine articles featuring the doctor look down on us from the walls. I don't want to say anything else out loud, for fear that the door will open at any minute and I'll be caught in a dramatic moment of *I cannot believe this lady* gossip.

Perhaps Mila feels the same because she doesn't say anything, either.

Finally, the doctor returns with a pep in her step and no apologies.

"Oh, and I'm also your therapist while you're my patient," she chirps. "Something I don't mind at all. I just do a little hand-holding here and there."

What the…? I think, still not saying anything in return.

She motions for me to stand. "Let's take a look at you now."

I untie the sash, underwear still on, and reveal my still-undergoing-chemo, childlike body.

"Ok, looks like we could get an A-cup out of you if we go that route," she says as she quickly assesses me with her eyes. Then, before I have a chance to ask any questions, she says, "Get dressed and I'll meet you down the hall in my scheduler's office."

"Wait…" I say to her back that is already exiting the room.

"I'll step out while you change," Mila says and exits as well.

When we walk back to the waiting room, where nearly all the chairs are full, the doctor is already there, center stage with all her disciples. She spots me and waves me to her side before a woman in her late thirties or early forties, saying, "This one has Stage 0 cancer—a carcinoma—and is willing to talk to you about her experience…"

I catch the patient's eyes with an apologetic smile, wondering, *Do we really have overlap in our experiences here? What does Stage 0 even mean?* She appears to be minding her own business, waiting for her appointment, not this forced intimacy.

Before we can speak to each other, though, the doctor hands me a notecard filled with writing.

"Here are the names of three other patients and their phone numbers who you may also speak to about their experiences."

I take the paper. The doctor then turns on her heel for her next appointment and leaves us. I thank the patient but am unable to engage further because the scheduler, whose office is adjacent to us, signals me over to the empty chair at her desk.

Mila, still on the periphery, calls to me quietly, "I'll wait for you," and points outside.

I give her a nod, longing to join her as the phrase, *I'm a celebrity, get me out of here!* booms in my head.

Instead, I move to the scheduler's desk.

"Oh, look at that," the scheduler says, looking at her computer, not at me, as I take a seat. "We are all booked out already for July… Then the doctor is traveling… Hmm, I could get you on the waitlist?"

Turns out everyone around here is more adept at making assumptions than asking me what I even want. I hold my breath. *Thank goodness nothing is available!*

"How about I just give you a call, shall I wish to move forward?" I manage to say, grateful that some part of my mind is still able to function—and has my back.

"Of course." She hands me a sheet with her details.

I don't know if I'm more pleased that I kept my tone polite or that I get to walk outside to rejoin Mila. But the freedom to be out of that space feels monumental and, to regain the parts of me I lost along that in-person query, I nap the rest of the day.

As the week goes on, I start to second-guess myself. *Have I misread something? Were my sensors malfunctioning during that visit?* I wonder, unable to understand the positive attention she's received.

I still have the notecard and, to clear my muddled thoughts, I call and leave messages for the three listed patients.

Every single one of them calls me back.

And every single one of them shares with me that they've had an infection or some sort of complication during or after their surgery. And yet, they go on and on about how *she is such a good friend, though!*

That settles it. I decide they are all completely brainwashed and I am not voluntarily signing up for an infection, harvesting my own tissue, or bigger breasts.

It really is no use trying, Imogen, in a space where your voice isn't accounted for—much less heard—and someone else's trajectory is so far off course from anything you imagined. And yet, this highlighting of what I don't want starts to align me with what I do want.

11 | sold

I call the male plastic surgeon next. To my surprise, he is the complete antithesis to the female one. From the moment I meet him, I am ecstatically at ease.

"I'd like an over-the-muscle surgery—with no spacers, please—keeping my B-sized cup," I tell him.

He starts, "Doctors prefer to do the surgery under the muscle these days because…" *Blah blah blah.* I tune him out. "…but I can and will do the surgery over the muscle for you, no problem," he finishes. Music to my ears.

He rolls his chair over to a drawer and pulls out two implants for me to hold and feel. *Helpful,* I think.

"This is saline," he explains, placing one in my hands. "If it leaks, it is nontoxic, but it has less of a natural look and feel."

I move it between my fingers and hand it to Mila, who is with me again.

"The silicone, you can tell, feels much more natural." He places the next sample in my hands. "There actually isn't much greater of a risk anymore; it is just recommended they be switched out and replaced every ten years."

It does feel more natural.

He leaves the room to gather some pictures for me.

As the door shuts, I say to Mila, "Oh my gosh, this is going so much better already!"

"I agree! I feel it, too!" she adds, and we share a burst of enthusiasm, grabbing each other's hands for a brief squeeze and shake.

The surgeon returns with a laptop to show us pictures of past patients who've consented to share and whose faces are absent. A quick glance gives the proof-of-concept my brain needs: Most of them chose silicone, and their breasts look very natural. I raise my hand and say, "Thanks, I'm good. I like the silicone better."

He further explains that, with reconstruction, he will remove all the breast tissue before he places the implants and then they will test the cells around the nipples during surgery. Their goal is to keep my nipples, but if pathology finds anything precancerous or cancerous there, the nipples will be removed.

It takes all of my willpower not to bring my hands to my mouth in shock. I hadn't even thought about that.

My reaction also tells me I'd prefer to have breasts than be left with a scar across my chest.

I hope my simple nod in reply indicates my maturity.

He tells me nipples can also be reconstructed in a separate surgery or tattooed on, which look very realistic. While I imagine this is a beautiful option for some, my insides reject it as a possible experience to add to my list. And yet, the surgeon reminds me that all of these are real risks and out of his control.

I focus instead on his compassion and candidness, let out the breath I've again been holding in, and thank him—desperately hoping we'll never have to have this conversation again.

And anyway, I am sold. I feel comfortable and understood.

It is easy to move forward, easy to get on his schedule, and easy to give this doctor my complete trust. I even look forward to the surgery—something I didn't imagine possible.

My mom flies out to be with me for my surgery. It's 6:00 a.m. when we arrive at the hospital.

After I'm prepped, I'm tucked into an alcove, behind a curtain, and the light around me is dim. My mom settles into the waiting room a few walls away and I'm thinking about how nice it is that I'm lying here at the very start of the day, still sleepy and not anxious.

"Knock knock," I hear my plastic surgeon say.

"Come in," I say.

He pulls the curtain aside and stands next to me. "I have one last question for you."

"Okay."

"Depending on the amount of tissue removed and the area I have to work with for the implant size, would you prefer to be a little smaller than your current size, or a little bigger?" He pauses. "*If* it came to that."

I let out a laugh. "I'd be okay with being a little bigger."

"Okay, great," he says. Even without my contacts in, I can tell he is smiling.

"One more thing?" I ask.

He remains beside me, focused on my face.

"Really, if you could keep my nipples, that would be my preference." I hold in my breath, proud of myself, even though my worry is still there.

"Yes, that is my goal as well," he says, and my chest falls in release.

It hurts to raise my head, much less sit up. *This is new*, I think. *It must be over.*

I am alone, and it is quiet.

Suddenly, I have to urinate—badly. A nurse comes in, hearing my rustling. "Hi, sorry to bother you," I quickly say, "but

I really have to pee and can't move."

"Hang on, I'll get a bedpan for you," she says, then steps out of the room.

OMG. How long is she going to be?

I am embarrassed but at a loss. I can no longer hold it and release my pelvic muscles to a gush of warm liquid that collects beneath me.

When the nurse returns a few minutes later, my cheeks burn. "I apologize. I couldn't wait. The sheets are all wet."

Even without seeing her exact expression, I can tell she is perturbed.

"I'll need to get someone to help me move you to another bed," she says with a sigh. "We were going to do that anyway—when we moved you to your room… Let me go see if it's ready." She turns to leave again.

"Wait," I say. "Could you please just tell me one thing first?"

"Sure." She moves nearer to me.

The surgery is over. I have to know.

"Can you tell me, do I still have my nipples?"

"Oh. I don't know," she says and steps closer, softening her shoulders. "But we can find out." She places her hands above my gown. "May I?"

"Yes, please."

Lifting the wrapping, she quickly peeks under my bandages. "Yes." She smiles, then tucks everything back in.

I smile back.

When she leaves the room, I lie there in my cold, wet sheets, luxuriating in this news, and send a silent note of gratitude to the upper world.

12 | a swim in the river

ost-chemo and post-op, I am on a high (off all drugs, mind you), not sweating the small stuff, and wanting to leap into a clear, abundant, refreshing beginning. I am ready for commitment, forward motion, elation.

Mark's timing, however, is a bit different from my own. This becomes challenging—mostly insofar as there is no doctor telling me what steps I need to take to get to a future together quicker, or how and when things will all work out.

I just have to live through it.

In the meantime, I begin my master's program—studying, drafting, drawing—and I learn how to hand-render three-dimensional objects and spaces in perspective. I use colored pencils in a new way and fall in love with watercolors. I get really into the sustainable systems and materials a building can offer and become a LEED-certified Green Associate.

I get back into running again with my friends. When I walk down the hill to meet them in the Marina district, as the warm Northern California glow hugs the tops of the eucalyptus trees goodnight in the Presidio to my left, I pinch myself, thinking, *This time is really special and fleeting.*

And in sessions with the shaman, I sink into a solid dose of upper world energy, the room illuminates, and I loosen my metaphorical grip on any expectations that I still cling to.

It isn't until two years later, in December 2012, that Mark and I finally make it to South Africa. We visit his family's holiday home on the river with his parents, his sister, her husband, and their young daughter, as well as his gran. I am struck by how the wilderness near Saint Francis Bay looks like the plains of Colorado. Even though there is an odd acacia tree, the colors and shrubs feel so familiar and homelike that it is hard to believe we are on the other side of the world.

The single-story space is minimal, and one day, we congregate under the covered front porch on plastic lounge chairs with cushions that have been brought out of storage for our stay. We look onto an open meadow surrounded by long saligna gum trees, with a well-trodden path around a bend leading down to the river.

"Will you go for a swim in the river?" Mark's family wants to know, already in their suits, ready to be relieved of the summer heat and jump in themselves.

"I think so…" I reply, unsure as to why I wouldn't.

This seems like a rite of passage test I need to do before being wholeheartedly accepted by Mark's family. This is because Mark has an American aunt who outright refuses to swim in this river. But, knowing there aren't crocodiles or fish that can hurt me, I agree to change and jump in.

The water is freezing. But I don't find it scary, even though I can't see the bottom. There is a calm, relaxed movement to the current. Mark's grandmother is in, too. *If she can wade in at her age and float so calmly, so can I!* I think, wondering why I felt hesitant.

I get the grand tour of Mark's early life when we stay at his childhood home a few days later, and just before the weekend, we secure a local's discount for an overnight stay at a game farm, about an hour north.

Upon our arrival, we are startled by—then quickly in awe of—the majestic presence of a bull elephant eating grass, camouflaged by some tall plants near the building's entry. Shortly after we put our bags down, we hop onto an open-air Land Cruiser for a drive around the sixty-two-thousand-acre reserve.

We see white rhino, zebra, and a napping male lion. We come across a Cape leopard in a tree, spot some wild boar, and are escorted off the vehicle to take some photographs beside two cheetahs lying in the shade of a wide shrub.

It is incredibly wonderful to be standing so close to these animals in their element—checking my fear in sharing their home with them—beside a knowledgeable guide. Walking these grounds really gives me a feeling of what it means for Mark to be African: aware of nature and in touch with his surroundings in a more meaningful way than just stepping out of a home mindlessly in a relatively safe and manufactured city like I'm used to.

But the moment that captivates me the most is when a journey of giraffes languidly moves across the horizon line at sunset, to the song of frogs, on our drive back to the lodge for dinner.

Mark's hand grabs mine as we witness nature's cinematic expression, and I think, Imogen, *Once I finally let go of the need for a fairy tale, the fairy tale appeared.*

At the end of 2013, Mark and I move into an apartment together on the lower floor of a butter-yellow Edwardian built in the 1900s. Among its charming built-in bookshelves and intricate crown molding, the space has a lovely back garden hosting a myriad of flowering bushes, a Japanese maple, and a crab apple tree.

A couple of weeks later, when the place is starting to feel like ours, I wake up to Mark down on one knee, next to my side of the bed, proposing. Of course, I say yes.

That same day, eager to make plans and thrilled to have carte blanche to do so, I book a date for a justice of the peace to marry us the following month. Since we've spent time with both of our extended families in the last year, we set aside our funds for the different-from-many childbearing journey we anticipate ahead, rather than a large ceremony.

Because the only way we know how to prevent cancer for future generations is to not pass on my BRCA1 gene.

But how is that done? Is it worthwhile?

It's time to find out.

part II | *with you*

Back at the IVF clinic, I'm not entirely at ease. Suddenly, being closer to getting pregnant feels like a big decision. The doc pulls out a blank sheet of paper and sets it on his desk in front of where I sit.

"With your dad being a carrier of BRCA1 and your mom not being a carrier," he starts, "you have two copies of this gene—one affected and one unaffected." He draws a rudimentary graphic with one squiggly line—the affected copy of the gene—and one straight line, the unaffected copy. Under both lines he writes *Lindsay* and circles my name. "Mark, on the other hand, has two unaffected copies of this gene."

He adds another drawing to the page with two straight lines and Mark's name circled underneath it. "When you fertilize an egg, whichever copy of the gene Mark passes on will be unaffected."

He draws another circle below ours, labeled *embryo*, with one straight line above it. "Now, as you can see, there is a fifty-fifty chance that you will pass on an unaffected gene as well."

Then he draws a line from under my name with the one squiggly line and the one straight line to indicate it is random which one will appear beside Mark's straight line in any fertilized embryo of our making.

"Therefore, we won't need Mark's DNA to isolate the gene under a microscope but will require yours and your father's to build a test. This will help the lab see if the genetic makeup of the embryo matches that of the inherited BRCA1 mutation you carry, or not."

"Wow," I say. "How is that done?"

"Copies of the specific DNA segments containing the BRCA1 gene are amplified so that the region of the mutation is detectable. This is part of a process called preimplantation genetic testing, or PGD."

Amazing. I can hardly believe this is possible.

"That being said," he looks at his computer screen then continues, "I'd like to get you in an exam room to see how your ovaries are looking. Even though you have some eggs and embryos frozen, our best options moving forward would be to do another retrieval of eggs to fertilize."

Oh. Hearing that surprises me. I wonder if he saw me react, then I notice his eyes are still glued to his screen.

He continues, "That way, you will have more probability of a healthy embryo or embryos to choose from on Day 5."

I feel a pressure in my mind building—the added expenses, the added time I didn't anticipate. The added ambiguity.

"Okay, wow, I didn't think I needed to do another round of IVF," I finally say out loud.

His eyes are back on mine. "Well, since we did your retrieval during a stressful time with a sense of urgency, I'm not quite certain how good the quality of the eggs and embryos are that we froze."

What? I think. *What does that mean? I didn't know I had to worry about that.*

He adds, "We froze them on Day 3, too, so we know less

about them."

"What is the difference between Day 3 and Day 5 again?" My dad has gone over this with me before, but this is the first time the distinction feels worth remembering, and I want to regain some footing here.

He flips over the paper and roughly draws some circles to indicate how cells start to divide after fertilization. For Day 3, he draws three circles within a circle and notes they can only tell a little bit about the quality of the embryo and test for gender at this stage, but not much else.

He draws even more circles within a circle for a Day 5/6 embryo and thickens the outer line of the largest circle they rest within and labels that outer line *placenta*.

"Once the embryo gets to the blastocyst phase at Day 5/6, we can retrieve cells from the outside layer that will become the placenta. These cells match the genetic makeup of the interior cells which will become the fetus, giving us much more information."

"Gotcha."

"It is from a sample of the placenta cells on this outer layer of a Day 5/6 embryo that we do PGD testing. We can also test for any other chromosomal abnormalities, like Down syndrome."

"Okay, wow, that certainly sounds helpful."

"If an embryo makes it to Day 5, it is more likely to carry to full term, too, with less chance of miscarriage, because of the properties of the cells they are able to read in the lab."

"All right, so Day 5 equals more promising, as far as an embryo goes."

The doctor then moves to the bottom quarter of the page to draw one more diagram.

"Let's imagine we start with twenty embryos," he says, drawing a bunch of tiny circles to indicate each embryo. "On Day 3, less of them will be dividing." He then draws an arrow to another bunch of tiny circles, showing maybe ten left. "And on Day 5/6," he says, drawing another arrow to the right and stopping at a group of about five circles, "there will be even fewer embryos dividing."

That is quite the visual.

Why didn't I consider these probabilities before?

As I stare at the sheet, he adds, "That is just how nature works. As you age, we have fewer eggs to work from. A diminished ovarian reserve is more prominent at age thirty-five."

Fuck me. I am already thirty.

"For some reason, I thought that happened at forty?" I tell him as all this data begins to pool in my brain.

Rather than restating what, to him, is obvious, he rattles off a few more facts and then completes his argument:

"After PGD testing there will be even fewer embryos remaining because we'll know which..." he hovers over the five little circles on the sheet, "are not carriers of BRCA."

Then his pen draws an added ring around *diminished ovarian reserve* and underlines *age 35.*

God, the pressure.

"I'd just like to increase the chances of you and Mark having healthy embryos to transfer," he says when he sets down his pen and encourages me to pocket the paper.

I want to leave it right there on the table, along with all of these implications. But I tuck it into my bag anyway. So he knows I heard him, I reiterate, "Got it. More embryos equal more options."

"Great," he says, then stands. "Let's have a look to see if your ovarian function has returned." He steps out of his office into the hall and gestures to the restroom at the end of it. "Go empty your bladder, then I'll meet you in exam room number 2."

How is it that there is still more information to uncover, Imogen? There are layers to IVF that a patient doesn't get up front, nor has much time to process.

Just as I am closing the door to the bathroom, I feel a vise grip return: that of a ticking time bomb I thought I'd already detonated.

Here I am, nearly married, having overcome a really big change in the trajectory of my life, and mentally ready to start a family the seemingly "right" way so I don't pass on cancer—and more hoops appear!

Hoops I didn't see coming.

Will I ever get to see these things coming? How many more will there be?

I let out a breath as I wash my hands.

You won't know until you're in it, I tell myself. And experiential learning like this is a lot to catch up with. A lot to handle. But, truthfully, also how I roll.

I look in the mirror and my mind keeps going, trying to make sense of how what I've already done for fertility preservation might have been for nothing.

Enough. I don't want to backtrack. I don't want to waste any more time.

In Room 2, I undress from the waist down. I place my folded clothing on a chair, hiding my underwear in the layers, then perch on top of the paper pulled over the patient table. I lift the folded sheet provided and open it up to drape over my legs and tuck around my bottom.

My pale ankles protrude from fuzzy socks, wiggling above the metal platform below. *Funny looking,* I think, about my feet being covered, and then, *Thank goodness I kept my socks on.* It is cold.

I look up when there is a knock on the door.

The doc enters along with a nurse, who readies the ultrasound equipment and wheels it nearby. A condom-like protector is placed over the probe to be inserted vaginally. I lie down and place my feet in the stirrups.

"Slide down a little further, off the edge," the doctor directs as he adjusts the bright end of a white snake lamp to shine between my knees.

Ugh, being on display like this never gets easier, I think as I scoot.

"You might feel a little pressure," he reminds me before the probe is in, looking around.

A grainy black-and-white image of my uterus fills the screen mounted on the wall above our heads. Some measurements are read aloud by the doc and typed in by the nurse. I see that a black round circle on one side is larger than one on the other side.

"I can't believe it!" the doc says with a wide smile. "It looks like your ovaries have plumped right back up!"

I feel an elation I hadn't anticipated, in response to his own.

"On one side more than the other, as you can see…" He points out my left and right ovaries on the screen. "But there is definite functionality there."

Taking in his enthusiasm, I feel he is a few steps ahead of me—ready for round two—but I still have some mental catching up to do. Had I known this was going to be such a revealing appointment for our future, I would've insisted Mark join me.

"If we were to go for another retrieval, what would the timing look like for the genetic testing?" I ask when fully clothed and sitting back in my doctor's office.

"Well, we would need to build the test first. My genetic counselor can get in touch to go through it all with you—which lab to use and what is needed for the test. This isn't something we do internally."

Oh, man. Another genetic counselor. I instantly deflate thinking about this person as the gatekeeper for our next step.

"When we know the timeframe of when the test will be ready, we can begin preparing you for a retrieval. At that time, we can thaw your previously frozen embryos and eggs—fertilizing those too?" he asks, I nod, and he continues: "and then grow them all out to Day 5/6. Of the embryos still dividing, we will extract a sample to test, after which they will be frozen until we have the results and you are ready for a separate frozen embryo transfer, or FET as we call it."

I press my fingers into my temples, then say, "I'll talk everything over with Mark and let you know."

I start unloading on Mark as soon as he walks in the door that evening.

"My ovarian function returned! I didn't even think about how detrimental it could've been if it hadn't—but it's there! I've never seen the doc so animated… Oh, and he wants to do another retrieval. Being thirty, I guess it's better now than later…"

I hardly take a breath, rambling on, recounting the many important points of the day. I pull out the doctor's drawings, making sense of them again with Mark as my audience.

I'd forgotten about the additional diagram showing how I'm born with the greatest number of eggs I'll ever have. I point to it, continuing my monologue, "He said that by forty, I'll have a minimal number of eggs left in good standing—that there is a cliff at thirty-five I didn't realize—and he'd like to have a greater pool of embryos to test from." I keep going, almost manic. "It could also take a while to build the test? I'm not sure. If we proceed trying not to pass on the gene, there will be some time needed for that."

Mark listens, then chimes in, adding his own pressing feelings: "I want to be a fit, agile father! And present! The sooner the better. And, really, if we are able to take away any worry for our children about having cancer or their children having cancer, we should do that, shouldn't we?"

"I think so. We are so fortunate to have this opportunity— and the ability to say yes. What a gift to be able to give to our children, and society, really."

"So true."

Being seven years older than me, his additions make sense and contribute to my own building urgency.

14 | the controls of procreating

To get things going, Mark and I meet with my IVF doc's genetic counselor in the middle of our work day the following week. I wish I could say I was pleasantly surprised by her demeanor but instead instantly detect a nervous energy that comes with youth and inexperience, similar to the previous genetic counselor.

"Hi, welcome, welcome—please take a seat," she says.

We sit. She shuffles some papers, not making eye contact. I'm sure my collapsed shoulders and expression are not easy to contend with for her part. Mark's energy feels much kinder and forgiving by my side (then again, he wasn't with me the last time) and I am grateful for his presence, for all our sakes.

"Okay, Lindsay, can I please get your family history…"

What, you don't have a cheat sheet? I think, already frustrated. I force myself to take a breath and repeat what I hope is already listed somewhere in front of her, rather than being confrontational.

"And Mark, being from South Africa," she says when I'm done, "do you or your family have any history of sickle cell disease?"

"No." He now also has a thin smile.

"What about any history of AIDS?"

"No."

Is she getting to you yet? I wonder, turning my head to Mark.

"And, any worry of having AIDS?"

Oh. My. Fucking. Goodness.

"No," he confirms.

"Okay, great," she says.

I let out a breath.

"Well, we'll need labs done anyway from both of you—as protocol—but Lindsay, we'll require a blood sample from your father, too, which states here he is the carrier of the gene, yes?"

Finally, it appears she is reading her paperwork.

"Yes."

"And we need saliva samples from both of your parents, which I'll give you the paperwork for."

"Okay."

She then gives us a refresher course on the BRCA gene with a printed-out PowerPoint that ends with a few options of labs to build the test, all running on different schedules. I ask for one they've worked with before with the quickest turnaround time, antsy to get on with it.

"We'll go with this one, then, that is six to eight weeks out," she tells us. "The others are taking two to four months."

"Gosh, that seems long." I recalibrate the timing in my head, crossing out the few weeks at most I'd assumed this would take. "But great, thanks," I add, remembering this probably isn't a one-off meeting.

The genetic counselor ends our session, saying she'll inform the doc and his care team of our decision and will be in touch again soon.

And what better way to wait than to wed? Mid-December, Mark and I marry on a clear, fresh, bluebird day. Our jackets are pulled up tight around our necks and our breath is visible in the cold air as we walk from the Civic Center parking lot to City Hall.

I hold a bouquet crafted by a friend that highlights a king protea in honor of South Africa, which she pulled next to a central pink rose in honor of my paternal grandmother. Mark's oldest brother, my parents, and Mila stand across from us under the majestic rotunda as our witnesses.

We enjoy some bubbly, beautiful bottles of Ridge wine and a catered meal at our new apartment afterward with them and a handful of our closest friends, enfolding each other in celebration and laughter.

A couple of weeks later, we fly to Maui for a makeshift honeymoon with some friends. We each stay in our own condos and meet up for meals, swims, and sightseeing.

There is a bay full of turtles we can walk to and, in swimming there, I quickly learn that Mark is very at home in the water and I am not. I slip at the rocky entry, freak out when I am very spaciously sandwiched between two large turtles—and clamber over Mark's back trying to get out. I am thankful I can send a friend to join Mark in my place.

Nevertheless, when we return to San Francisco, I feel sun-kissed and reset for the new year, 2014.

When our IVF clinic's lab reopens after the holidays, I call our genetic counselor for an update on timing. She doesn't have one but promises to get back in touch once she does. I sigh—a few times—thinking this is going to take more patience than I realized.

Once it's been eight weeks *after* the holidays and I *still* haven't heard anything, nor received any further indication on timing from our counselor, I look up the number of the lab itself and call them directly.

It is really easy for me to get a hold of someone regarding my case. After a few security questions validating my identity as the patient, I am passed along to a coordinator who tells me they haven't started yet. *Uh, whoops!* My emotions do a one-eighty. I take a breath and ask if she has an idea of when they'll be able to begin.

"Yes. It looks like another two to four months."

What. The. Fuck.

My heart sinks with disappointment and rage starts to fill my insides. But I do have the wherewithal to not kill the messenger, so give her a polite "thank you for letting me know," and hang up.

Phew, Imogen, putting the controls of procreating in the hands of others and their timelines is much more emotionally challenging than I would wish for anyone.

But I have the news now and need to see if there is another place available to build our test, sooner. This becomes my call-to-action. Within a few hours, I've gotten ahold of our genetic counselor and she's found another lab that has the availability to start immediately with an under eight-week turnaround.

The outside lab emails me when our test is complete.

Hall-le-fucking-lu-jah!

Time to take the reins and charge ahead.

15 | olive tree hypothesis

I call the IVF clinic and am put through to the care team for my doc. I proudly share that I've been waiting for a genetic test to be built, because I'm a BRCA1 carrier, and that test is now ready.

"Okay," she says, and I hear her typing. "Looks like we'll need to get you in for an orientation that we do for all new patients first."

"Well, I'm not necessarily a new patient. I've had a retrieval with this doctor before," I tell her, hoping to bypass the general protocol and just get going.

"How long ago was that?"

"At the end of 2009."

"Well, since that was over four years ago, we need you to attend."

Oh-kaaay… I make a trilling noise at the back of my throat, wishing I could just barrel through all these requirements. "All right. Please put me down for the next one, then," I surrender. Again.

The orientation is in an auditorium filled with other couples about to embark on their infertility journeys.

Let me tell you, I don't think any of us want to be in that room together, seen by one another. It's enough that all these doctors know our innermost vulnerabilities to something that we thought should come to us naturally. Yes, our case is by choice, but it isn't like we're holding up a sign as to why—or are even ready for that at this stage. Nor, probably, is anyone else.

Thankfully, we don't come across anyone we know, and everyone keeps to themselves.

The presentation covers the whole gamut of fertility options. A lot of terminology we are familiar with is repeated, in detail. We learn about surrogates and gestational carriers and the probability of twins, due to the medications provided and/or the implantation of multiple embryos. This is the first time we hear the term *singleton* when the doctors mention it is safer to grow one fetus in a uterus, should an embryo split or multiples take. I hadn't stopped to consider the possibility of twins before and don't like being lumped into this pool of potential among a wider audience.

"Gosh, what do they do to the other fetuses?" I whisper to Mark as they pause significantly on these slides.

There is a specific medical reason given, but I just want to get out of here, now, feeling like this does not apply to us and that I don't want to take on the thoughts of these risks that other couples may need to take into account. It's more playing God than Mark and I need to consider.

My second retrieval arrives a few weeks later. After waiting months to kickstart this process, I feel in the zone and along for the ride.

"Congratulations!" the nurse whispers as I blink my eyes open in the recovery bay. "You had thirty-two eggs retrieved." She points to a number, again written on my hand.

"Whoa!" I respond, waking up, startled it is even higher than the first time around.

"Yeah, that is a great number."

"Thanks," I say and close my eyes, feeling into the soreness and smiling at the results.

Meanwhile, I will later hear, Mark, my doc, and my dad—in town again to be present for all things IVF—discuss the results in the waiting room. My dad mentions a research paper he recently came across—one that my doc is familiar with but did not author—describing an "olive tree hypothesis" post-chemotherapy. The hypothesis likens ovarian function returning to an olive tree post-pruning: The tree looks dead, appears it will not grow again, and then the leaves return and come back even more abundantly.

That evening, the embryologist calls with our fertilization report.

"We are starting with twenty-five embryos."

"Wow, that is wonderful—and feels like a lot." My eyes widen and I remember to ask, "That must include some of the embryos from my 2009 retrieval, right?"

My heart beats a little faster, anxious for the answer.

"No, actually. Unfortunately, none of the eggs or embryos from your 2009 retrieval survived the thaw."

What? I think, shocked. Instead, I voice a simple, "Oh."

I mean, what can I do about it now?

"Thank you for letting me know," I tell him.

"You're welcome. Speak to you again in a few days."

We hang up and I call my dad, now home, to keep him in the loop. I ask him about the eggs and embryos not surviving the thaw, and his only explanation is that they must've not been in good shape because of the high stress I was in at the time of the retrieval.

Ah, right.

On Day 5, one embryo reaches the blastocyst phase.

On Day 6, three more embryos make it to blastocyst.

Okay, amazing. I feel optimistic. We have four embryos to test.

They will be biopsied, then frozen, and we will receive the results within ten days.

A week later, an email from our genetic counselor appears in my inbox. My heart leaps to see *Results* in the subject line.

Thank goodness! I think. *Something in this process has happened faster than I anticipated!*

I now work full-time at a green construction company doing high-end home renovations, and it is the middle of the week, just after lunch, when many of the builders are still in the field and a few of us project managers are getting through paperwork. It is quiet in the office, so I quickly stand up from my desk to step outside and call her.

The heat of the sun warms my nerves as I open up the attachment on my phone and dial. Once she answers, she gets straight to it.

"As you'll see in the results, you have two healthy, well-graded embryos that are not carriers of BRCA1, nor have any chromosomal abnormalities..."

I walk uphill on the concrete sidewalk.

"Those two, we call *euploid*—having a normal number of chromosomes—and *not affected*, meaning BRCA1 is not in the genetic makeup."

I make it to the top of the street where the road ends and a valley of shrubs takes over beyond a parking lot.

"Great to hear, thank you, that makes sense."

I spot blooms on the lavender plants and patches of green grass poking through dusty gold tumbleweeds below. I feel a fullness emerge in me, hearing that two potential future children are available to us.

"You also have one additional healthy embryo—euploid—that *is* a carrier of BRCA1, so it is noted there as *affected*."

All right, as expected, there is at least one embryo with the gene, I think, as the wind blows a warm breeze and I turn to make my way back down to the office.

"Your fourth and final embryo is *not affected* yet is *aneuploid*, meaning it has an abnormal number of chromosomes, which increases risk of miscarriage, birth defects, and implantation failure. We don't recommend that one be transferred."

Hearing this—that one embryo is abnormal and would likely be miscarried—deflates me. Those words, out loud, are sad. *So strange to be given this information on paper,* I think. And yet, after all the discussion around odds earlier with my doc, there is already a slot in my brain for this news to slide into, for my mind to accept.

"Okay, thank you for talking me through this information," I say, looking over the results one more time.

"You're welcome."

My eye catches on some black rectangular boxes that she hasn't addressed.

"I have one question, before you go," I say. "Is that some sort of blacked-out information there, on the page, next to each embryo?"

"Yes. That is the gender, which has been masked, per your request."

Oh, yeah. I'd forgotten we didn't want to know that information.

Why had Mark and I requested the gender be kept from us?

We keep wondering.

"Maybe the two embryos are one boy and one girl," I say to Mila over the weekend, while Mark and I lounge with her on her deck overlooking Angel Island.

Pots of white bougainvillea frame the sailboats dotting the water in the distance. We have flutes of champagne in hand to celebrate our two BRCA-free embryos.

"What would you like them to be?" Mila asks, entertaining our thought exercise.

"Gosh, I always thought I'd have two boys," I admit. "Growing up, when I was a camp counselor—first for fifth graders as a high schooler in Colorado, then later, in college, at a camp in upstate New York—I just connected to the boys better. I could be more playful with them. There was less drama."

I go on to recall how the fourteen-year-old girls I bunked with kept me up all night with their homesickness and I had a hard time empathizing with their worries and attachment to things. I picture the Tiffany's charm bracelets they'd brought to camp and then stressed about losing—*why, WHY bring those to camp?*—and one girl in particular who crawled into bed with me to console her. Have me be motherlike. But I was nineteen and just wanted a good night's sleep.

The boys were easier to entertain, more immersed in the bliss of the moment, happier to hit a tennis ball back or be amused by songs and activities around a campfire at the lake.

"I would be happy with either," Mark chimes in.

Hearing Mark's openness—free of judgment or request—a part of me doesn't want to give up on the possibility of a girl because of my past experience. A part of me thinks she'd be like me and *that* is something, *someone*, I could connect with.

I enjoyed the girl in me who, rather than playing with her dolls, lined them up for photo shoots with disposable cameras, or wrapped up different trinkets for the thrill and surprise of unwrapping them. A girl who drew and read and could get lost in the hours of the day making "creations" with ice cream and toppings, secret potions with lotion and grapes, or columns of cartoon facial expressions that friends could mix and match to invent characters of their own.

What would my daughter's magical inner world be like?

"Yeah, if given the option," I add, "I'd love to have a girl, too." Saying this out loud gives a new part of me permission to open up in welcome and wonder.

Mila nudges a bowl of Marcona almonds toward us. My fingers collect a small handful and I drop a few into my mouth. The salty, oily crunch accompanies my daydreams as we keep pontificating, sipping cold, dry bubbles, and coming up with potential names for either a boy *or* a girl.

Perhaps if we'd stuck with the mystery of gender, my connection to you, Imogen, would be nonexistent and I wouldn't be here, sharing our story. Perhaps if we weren't living in this time of modern medicine, the knowledge of these kinds of choices wouldn't lodge somewhere deep in my psyche and bury there for years to come.

But something kept stirring in both me and Mark after receiving the results: a desire, a curiosity, a longing to have the gender of our embryos revealed.

Was that you?

Maybe it was because the more we thought about it, the more we knew that someone out there, in a lab somewhere, knew more about our potential future children than we did.

But I'd say, too, part of us—part of *me*—needed you to be known.

We make a plan to move forward with a frozen embryo transfer. Given the information we have to work with, I tell our doc that it is for either of the two healthy BRCA1-free embryos we have, regardless of gender.

But then, back in his office, sitting across from him, I push myself to ask, "By the way, *could* you tell us the gender of our embryos?"

An electricity quietly hums in my veins. I try to keep my legs still.

"Let me see…" he says, pulling up our results on his desktop computer. "Looks like that information is masked for me, too." He then looks over at me. "You'll need to call the genetic counselor."

Ah yes, not so fast, Lindsay—back to the gatekeeper. I grunt at the thought.

When I head out of the building, I fire off an email to her from my phone requesting the gender of our embryos be revealed. It auto-replies within seconds that she is on vacation. I scroll down, relieved to see a name and number I can call in her absence.

Before I step in the car, I quickly type in the number. My phone rings through to the lab as I buckle my seatbelt. After a quick security check, I am given the full unmasked information:

"Both of your unaffected chromosomally normal embryos are male."

My heart pounds as she continues.

"The two remaining—the embryo with BRCA1 and the aneuploid embryo—are female."

There you are. There. You. Literally. Are. My one healthy female embryo, and you have BRCA1.

This is our official introduction.

What do I feel?

Mixed emotions.

I am grateful for the opportunity to have two boys without BRCA1—and on the heels of my earlier declaration at Mila's, a part of me is not surprised by these results. But what I wasn't expecting was coming face-to-face with the potential of someone like me: female and with the BRCA1 gene. Nor was I expecting this as a byproduct of our choice—meaning choosing *not* to bring someone *like me* into the world.

Yes, this should've been obvious, but now arriving at this bridge, it is much harder to cross in a carefree way than at the genesis of our decision. There is no slot in my brain to instantly make peace with these facts.

I quickly rein my thoughts back to the blessings of our choice: for future generations, BRCA1 and BRCA1-related cancers will not be a worry for our BRCA1-free embryos. This still rings true as having tremendously powerful ramifications.

This is my touchstone. Here I am touching it.

Yet, I have an instant connection to you, Imogen, someone with my same lineage—not only half of my genetic makeup mixed with your dad's, but we share the gene that also helped me grow as a person.

I think of the shaman helping me to bring in the upper world and ground myself, which allowed me to remember not to make other people's thoughts and opinions "big stuff" that derails me—how to be clearer on my own inner voice. I think of my time during treatments and after, learning to be my own best friend, not needing or expecting that from a partner, but letting that need go so, in a way, it could show up—a time during which I also gained more creative tools and built female friendships. Like attracts like, remember? I think of how I've gotten to do SO. MUCH. ELSE. besides cancer and how cancer doesn't define me. How I just don't let it.

When people hear what I've been through, they often tell me, *I'm so sorry*, but I stop them there, saying, *It's okay, really*, because I have gained so much from this experience. What I don't tell them is that, if given the choice of whether or not to live, I'd choose this life every time.

Am I taking this same choice away from you?

Sitting outside in the sunshine on our back patio a few days before my next IVF appointment, I open up a popular young adult novel, *The Fault in Our Stars* by John Green. Not really knowing what I'm getting myself into, I learn, a few pages in, that the female protagonist is a teenager with cancer (not breast cancer, but cancer nonetheless).

The story gets to me right in the opening chapters. I am in her world and it is heart-wrenching. Pressure builds in my chest, my cheeks dampen, and tears make their way to my tongue. As my vision blurs, the sun brightens the words on the page and I pause, placing my hand on the paper. It feels too painful to sit with a desire for you.

I walk inside and share as much with Mark.

"Ugh, why are you reading that?" he asks.

"Because I feel so much love for this story," I say. "It pulls me in."

I keep reading, challenging myself and our touchstone. *Maybe I can't really know the answer*, I wonder, *not being a parent yet.*

But every few chapters, I think, *No, I don't want my own child to go through this.*

After I turn the last page that evening, I hug the book to my chest. I feel validated in our original goals: Given the choice, we won't pass on the potential for cancer to our future offspring and theirs.

I am grateful—for this opportunity, for this book—and ready to move forward with the already planned transfer of one of our two male embryos.

17 | a paid job

Mark and I attend an injection class to cover some new material, most notably that in *this* phase of in vitro— for a frozen embryo transfer (FET) and not a retrieval—I'll need to have progesterone-in-oil. Our biggest takeaway from the session is in the form of two large circles drawn in black Sharpie on the back of my hips.

"These indicate the target locations for your progesterone," the nurse explains, clicking her pen cap closed. "Patients find it better for their partner to give these injections because the needle is larger" (*yikes!*) "and when lying down, it is easier to relax the muscle when you can look away."

She taps the outer top of my bum, much like an instructor in a barre class that wants you to squeeze your muscle tighter, but with the opposite goal in mind.

"Relax this muscle," she says. "It will be much less painful. It also helps to rub the skin quickly, back and forth, at the injection site afterward. To warm the oil for quicker absorption."

"What if my partner is out of town?" I have a false grin on my face, already anticipating an upcoming week when I know Mark will be away for work. "What is the best way for me to do it myself—if I must?"

"You can lean up against the wall with the hip you're not injecting," she demonstrates. "Have the syringe already filled in your dominant hand and twist around to reach the opposite hip. Put pressure against the wall when you twist, so the outer hip relaxes."

I stare at her, committing her stance to memory.

"Swab the skin with an alcohol wipe and stretch the area with the hand not holding the syringe…"

I hold my breath.

"Then quickly jab the clean skin with the syringe and *slowly* push in the medicine."

I exhale audibly and think, *Please don't make me do a test injection.*

"We don't have any needles that you can use today to try it," she says, reading my mind, "but when you know it is what is keeping your embryo attached to your uterine lining before the placenta takes over *and* is what prevents you from miscarriage, you will do it."

"Well, when you put it that way…yes, I guess I will."

I sigh. This is feeling like a lot, ah-gain.

I'm kind of wishing I braved the alternative to the progesterone-in-oil injections: a three-times-a-day vaginal cream. I said no because I instantly thought of the jobsite I'm now on midday and the porta-potty as the only bathroom option to tend to this need (no thanks!). I already actively avoid it thanks to the burly men who frequent it after having their meat stew lunches (more no thanks).

The nurse hands me a list of what medicine to purchase from their online pharmacy, along with an extensive schedule of which patch to put on when, which injection to begin when, their duration, and the differing amounts required.

Mark and I leave with our gospel of paperwork in hand,

intent on redrawing those Sharpie circles like it's a paid job.

Before we know it, the fascinating sequence of preparing my body for pregnancy begins.

In brief: The Lupron—that I used during chemo to protect my ovaries—now suppresses my ovarian function so that no eggs release naturally. I take estrogen via a patch to thicken my uterine lining so it is ready to receive the transfer of our embryo in a few weeks' time. I'll start the progesterone injections during my natural ovulation cycle to keep my uterine lining thick to support implantation five to seven days later. These shots will continue for twelve weeks after implantation to make sure that the placenta takes over making progesterone. As things build and progress, I will be monitored at the fertility doctor's office for optimal implantation conditions.

There are a few moments, though, Imogen, when I find myself alone in the bathroom and overwhelmed by the entire process. Weighed down even further by hormones.

Is it weird—telling my body to be pregnant by injecting myself with this medicine? Am I forcing things? And even: Am I just having these feelings because of the medication I'm taking?

I want to be in control, not passing on the gene, but is this too much control? Too many variables involved? Will it even work out okay?

A part of me wants to give up—to just try naturally, roll the dice, see what comes. Because this all feels so unnatural, fueled by constant adrenaline that keeps me hyperaware so I don't mess anything up. This part of me carries a whisper of mourning, too, for not conceiving the way I always assumed I would.

At the same time, a larger part of me shouts that this is something to be celebrated! *Come on, Lindsay, be grateful for this privilege, this advancement, this incredible option!* All the exclamation points.

The highly orchestrated components make the steps feel loaded, yet there is a lightness and abundance tagging along, too, reminding me that there would be no guarantee of preventing future breast or ovarian cancer if we threw in the towel with IVF.

When these moments come, when all of this builds inside me, I blow out air and lie on the cold porcelain tile, angry and confused as to why this is on my shoulders and not on the insurance companies'. Why does it have to be *my* choice to do *this* work for society, given all that doctors know about the gene?

I stay there, unable to get up, until I hear a voice still encouraging me that IVF is the best decision given the information I have and what *is* in my control: *How hard is it, Lindsay, to get through this short-term pain for the long-term gain? Stop looking this gift horse in the mouth!* I chastise, then shake my shoulders, willing the heaviness to leave my body.

I remind myself often that there have been many other brave souls before me who have achieved success—*and* that I've been able to see this firsthand, growing up as an IVF doctor's daughter. I've met, and heard of, so many healthy babies and their families, overwhelmingly grateful for these children who wouldn't be here otherwise.

As surreal as it is, these options were crafted long before my time. I am not the first one, and I won't be the last. So, why does the journey feel so lonely?

Focused on the progressive intent behind all these helping hands and tried-and-true methods, I get myself up, wash my hands, and stay the course.

Transfer day is a Tuesday afternoon. I swallow a Valium and a glass of water, then leave the office after lunch. Mark and I arrive together at the doctor's office.

Not a lot of fanfare is required. I change into a gown, lie down on a table, and receive a palm-sized black-and-white picture of my thawed embryo "hatching."

In front of me is a wall of windows. The lab is behind them. A door opens and our embryo is passed to our doctor in a prepared tube (or catheter, rather). There is some checking of numbers to make sure it is ours.

Gosh, I don't even want to think of what would happen if this was a mix-up! I think, momentarily squeezing my eyes shut. *Ugh.* I sigh, ardently wishing this all goes well.

When I open my eyes back up, I see the doctor guiding the catheter into my uterus. He deposits the embryo, removes the tube, and the transfer is complete.

"All done," the doc says.

"That's it?"

"Yes, you're free to go."

Sitting up to re-dress, I'm not entirely confident that the embryo won't fall out. I've heard of other patients having this sensation before and laugh to myself that I'm now feeling it.

The nurse reassures me that I can get up and move around. Once home, the rest of the day is quiet.

Two weeks later, I walk into a clinic on the ground floor of the medical building near my old apartment—the same building where I had chemo and was told I was a BRCA1 carrier. This appointment—for a blood draw—is more hope-filled, the promise of a new life beginning inside me.

Would you like juice after the draw? the nurse asks.

Yes, yes I would.

How about a colorful Band-Aid?

Don't mind if I do. A soft smile shines through my eyes.

It is my birthday.

At my desk a few hours later, I receive a call with the news that I am pregnant.

The elation sits quietly inside me, surprising me sporadically, until I pick up Mark from the ferry in Larkspur after work, and it is free to be let out, shared, celebrated.

We eat at Picco, one of our favorite restaurants in Marin, to celebrate. The late June evening is warm, the light golden, and it feels like there is magic dancing in the air around us.

18 | crude drawings

The time arrives for me and the progesterone shots to have our showdown.

Mark flies to New York and I am home alone, staring at the oil and needles. The soreness post-injection has been hit or miss with Mark administrating them. I surmise this is because I'm over-twisting my hip or flexing the opposite glute muscle too dedicatedly in hopes of relaxing the one on the receiving end.

Nevertheless, it is the mental hurdle of puncturing the skin and anticipating the pain that is my very present barrier to action with the items laid out before me, filling an area smaller than my palm. I tell myself to focus on one step at a time—which, luckily, I have memorized from backseat-driving Mark's work.

I select a syringe base first and pull back the plastic wrap, keeping it sterile. I peel off the aluminum film from a larger needle and, with the plastic casing around the point, twist it onto the syringe. I set down the syringe, now with the needle attached, and pick up the oily vial of progesterone.

Okay, great, that was easy, I encourage myself as I pop off the little plastic lid, tear open an alcohol wipe, and brush it over the slick top of the squat reusable bottle.

Then I remove the plastic casing from the needle on the syringe and insert the beveled tip into the vial. *This one is just large because it draws up the medicine*, I remind my insides as the pounding of my heart increases.

I pull back the plunger to slowly draw the liquid up to the required cc measurement, then remove the needle from the progesterone and slowly push out a small bead of liquid to remove any air bubbles.

Once my ammo is loaded, I reapply the plastic casing to twist off the longer, wider needle and drop it in the sharps container before adhering a slightly shorter and narrower one to inject the medicine into my body.

I stare at it, holding it like a dart. *Okay, this is sharp so it enters more painlessly*, I tell myself and take a breath.

I unbutton my jeans with my left hand and fold the fabric down till I see the Sharpie outline on my upper outer hip. I split open another alcohol wipe with my teeth and run the cool, wet square over the tender terrain of purple and yellow bruises.

I twist my body some more to evaluate the area. *This is like serving in tennis*, I coach myself. *Pick a spot, aim, and commit.*

"You won't feel it, Lindsay. You won't feel it," I say out loud, willing my eyes to remain open. I home in on an unblemished patch of skin, move my hand forward with a flick, and push in the needle.

I take a deep breath and slowly press in the medicine, pausing before I withdraw. I then quickly rub the area with my left hand.

"Woo!" I shout. "I didn't feel a thing!"

And then I laugh—because that was actually less painful than having Mark do it.

I do most of the remaining injections myself.

"There is the head," the sonographer points out at my twenty-week scan, rolling the transducer around and clicking on her keyboard to capture images, "And the arms and legs…"

After weeks laden with fatigue and skirting around the news at work, but without the engorgement of breast tissue, it is deeply comforting to see limbs and a head with features forming a smile flash by on the screen in front of us.

"And you know your baby's gender already, yes?" She waits for us to nod. "Because there is his penis…" she says, pausing on that part of the baby before moving on.

"I hadn't really thought of a little penis growing inside me before," I say out loud with a smirk to Mark.

"I'm going to take a few more measurements," the sonographer continues, ignoring my comment. She clicks and types some more, then stops. "Okay, got it. Just wait here a moment. I'll be right back."

She steps out of the room, and I look over to Mark. He shrugs his shoulders.

We wait. Longer than feels comfortable.

Where did she go? I wonder, but before I can voice as much, she returns.

"I'm going to print your first baby pictures for you!" she says.

"Okay, thanks," I say neutrally, watching her like a hawk as paper peels out of a printer.

"And here, for your stomach." She hands me a wad of wet wipes she's pulled from a nearby container. "The hospital doctor is going to come review the results with you."

Huh. *Way to just slip that in there*, I think, feeling this is all a bit strange as I clear the gel from my abdomen.

After a knock on the door, a doctor enters. He greets us amicably, then gets to the point: "Your sonographer has detected a velamentous cord insertion, but we can't quite see where it attaches."

My mind tries but fumbles to repeat the words he just said.

"Sorry, what?" Mark asks.

"An abnormal placement of the umbilical cord—which could compromise the growth of your baby, given that it is not connecting directly to the placenta."

I elbow my way up to a seated position, considering this as I clasp my hands on my lap. "What does that mean, exactly?"

"It's hard to know at this point, but I'd recommend planning a Cesarean section to avoid an adverse outcome."

My eyes widen at Mark.

"We'll send these images over to your doctor and she'll review them with you at your next appointment, which will be in a couple of days, right?"

"Yes." I swallow my nerves and compose myself. "I'm seeing her the day after tomorrow."

"Okay, wonderful. You'll know more soon," he adds as if to comfort us, then says goodbye and makes his exit. But that was not at all comforting.

"What in the…" I say to Mark once we're walking down the corridor and out of anyone's earshot. "Adverse outcome? Does that mean death?"

These are rhetorical questions. Mark is just as in the dark as I am.

"Let's ask my dad," I say once we're outside. "See if he can possibly give us any more information."

At the car, with the call on speakerphone, my dad reasons with us that it isn't an emergency unless the doctors say it is (which they haven't). Given that he hasn't seen the scan and we don't have any further details, he tells us to sit tight. Try not to panic.

This feels impossible.

"The baby is growing well and along a normal trajectory," our obstetrician tells us two excruciating days later, "but there is something about a velamentous cord insertion that we need to watch."

She grabs a piece of paper, places it on her clipboard, and presents the blank sheet in front of me and Mark. We both look over as she draws the blobby shape of a fetus within a circle, and at the top of the circle, makes an extra thick line.

"Here is the baby," she says and points to the blob, "and this is the placenta." She points to the thickened line.

She then draws what looks like an umbilical cord off to the side of the placenta connecting with the uterus and explains, "A velamentous cord insertion is when the umbilical cord does not feed directly into the placenta, but to the membrane off to the side, lining the uterus."

"Ohhhh," I say as the meaning finally clicks.

"That is why it puts your pregnancy in a more high-risk category—because the cord is not protected. Extreme pressure, like what happens in birth, can rupture the connection prematurely. This is why the doctor at the hospital may have indicated this setup can be detrimental to the baby's survival."

Mark and I slowly nod, digesting these risks we didn't even know to think about.

"This only becomes a matter of whether or not to have a C-section delivery if the cord is attached to the membranes near the birth canal."

She pauses. I keep hold of her eyes and wait.

"In your latest scan, they couldn't determine where the cord was connecting, so I will order another one to take a closer look. If the cord is connected up toward your abdomen, we can still try for a vaginal delivery."

"Okay, that is something," I manage to give her, even though I'm not really sure which is more daunting to me: a vaginal birth or a C-section.

"There is no immediate threat," she reiterates. "This is just more information so we can plan accordingly."

"Okay." I inhale. "Great." I exhale.

"But, do realize that being pregnant through IVF already puts you in a high-risk category. We'll be monitoring you more anyway toward the end of your pregnancy."

"Oh, goodness." *Why didn't anyone tell me this before?* I wonder, sinking in my seat, starting to feel not cut out for pregnancy at all.

"Hang tight a sec," she tells us and steps out of the room.

She returns quickly, wheeling in a rudimentary ultrasound machine with a speaker but no screen; later, I learn this is called a fetal doppler. She pops a probe onto my abdomen and we all immediately hear a rapid *tha-thump tha-thump tha-thump*.

"There. Listen to that!" Her face lights up. "That is a strong heartbeat."

My eyes heat as Mark and I share a wobbly smile with one another, our own racing hearts softening.

On the way home, I clutch the doctor's crude drawing with fervent hope.

19 | pressure

Mid-January, my sister is in town for my baby shower. We're in the bathroom getting ready before meeting up with my running club for a walk along Crissy Field, followed by brunchy snacks and gifts at a friend's house. My sister is curling my hair—a practice as effortless for her as brushing her teeth and one I've only done a handful of times.

"You're looking a bit puffy," she comments.

Having given birth to two babies herself, I examine my appearance with curiosity, rather than offense. After receiving the good news at my next ultrasound that the baby's umbilical cord was connected to the top of the placenta and not in danger of rupturing at birth, I've been appreciating a healthy, manageable pregnancy, not stopping to look too closely.

But in the mirror, I see the fullness of my cheeks; then, careful not to jerk my head with her holding the hot iron, I look down at the thickness of my ankles.

"Hmm, maybe that is just what is supposed to happen?" I notice in agreement, recalling a previous coworker's story in which her feet grew half a size during pregnancy and she was no longer able to wear her favorite shoes.

"Maybe," she says.

On our walk, the air is crisp and the sky a deep cerulean blue with a few vibrant white clouds. The breeze whips the smell of the sea around our faces as we stroll to the base of the Golden Gate Bridge and back.

At the shower afterward, my friend hands me welcome slices of both lemon and chocolate cake. As I take the plates with a happy *Why not, I'm pregnant, thank you very much!* grin, another dear friend, who is also pregnant and has an older child, takes note of my round cheeks and thick ankles. She kindly mentions it to me as an aside, with a knowingness that it isn't from being overserved.

"Everything okay?" she asks.

"I think so," I say as we lean into each other to smile for a picture, my fork midair.

This friend of mine is so slender, I chalk it up to different body types, thinking my water retention must just be part of the deal for me. Maybe even more so because I am pregnant through IVF. I don't know. But these thoughts ruminate in my mind throughout the afternoon.

Back home later, my sister and I call my dad to see if I should be concerned.

"Just lie down and stay off your feet for the rest of the day," he advises. "See if the swelling goes down by the morning. It should."

I do and it does.

I start my maternity leave at thirty-five weeks. I am large—my feet continuing to swell, off and on, always alleviating by morning, and my face still full—but not uncomfortably so. However, I am ready to be done smelling varnishes and avoiding airborne debris from various jobsites. I don't have a direct conversation with my supervisor about when or in what capacity I'll return, but I already know I'd like to be the one with my baby as he grows, rather than relinquishing the entirety of my salary for a stranger to do the same. In unspoken terms, we leave things loose.

The first Saturday of my leave arrives overcast and chilly in the city. Mark and I head over the bridge midday in search of warmth and fish and chips. The fog still hovers in Sausalito, but to appease my immediate hunger, we park, grab our coats, and find a picnic table outside a small "sustainably-sourced seafood eatery."

As we devour our lightly fried, flaky cod, we notice some rambunctious children carelessly running around on the dock below, dangerously close to the water's edge. We raise our eyebrows in silent cahoots like *Those will not be our children*, smugly unaware that we have no clue what parenting actually entails.

Imogen, let me tell you, no one really knows what any of this is like until they are in it. Pregnancy, birth, parenting—you have to just figure it all out moment to moment.

When I get into bed that night, I pull off my socks and notice my ankles are puffy again, but this time, *really* puffy. I point them out to Mark, entertained by their foreign shape.

"Uh, those are really swollen," he says, pressing his fingers into my skin, searching for bone.

"Yeah. Maybe it was the salty food?"

"Maybe you should call your dad."

"Nah…let's give it the night to see if the swelling goes down." I remove my feet from our scrutiny and tuck them under the covers. "Not much he can tell us right now."

I'll rest up, like he directed before, and see what happens.

I doze off into a fitful sleep.

My dreams are ridden with anxiety. Am I falling? Or in a car crash?

I wake with a gasp. I realize it's the middle of the night, then close my eyes again only to fall back into the same dream. I feel the same stress when I come to. My eyes blink open. It's still dark out.

I roll over and close them for a third time, thinking the dream is behind me and I'll finally get some rest. Within a few breaths, I'm back in the exact same scene, on repeat. My heartbeat is pounding and won't settle. *This is weird*, I think, but I am so tired that I don't move.

Before I know it, I startle awake again and the sun is rising. *Great, I don't have to go back to sleep*, I say to myself, but my heart is still racing.

I pull back the covers to look at my ankles. They're still thick, if not thicker.

I call my dad.

"Hey Beetle," he answers—his term of endearment for me.

Mark stirs beside me when I start to speak.

"Dad, I just woke up. My ankles are still really swollen from yesterday *and* I had the same recurring stress dream all night," I squeeze out, hardly taking a breath. "I'm feeling really anxious."

"Let me talk to Mark," he replies calmly. "Just stay in bed. Try to relax and keep your feet up."

His wanting to talk to Mark, though, isn't calming for me to hear. I immediately think he is shielding me from something. *What is going on?*

I hand the phone to Mark, who is now up and alert.

"Do you have a blood pressure cuff at home?" I overhear my dad ask.

"No."

"Okay, do me a favor and go to the nearest twenty-four-hour Walgreens. Pick up a blood pressure cuff, take Lindsay's blood pressure, then call me with the results. Tell Lindsay to stay in bed and rest."

This springs Mark into action. When he returns twenty minutes later with a digital blood pressure reader, I sit up and he straps it to my upper arm. He pushes a button, it squeezes, and I jot down the numbers in my Notes app.

"Whew, I think those are high," I say.

We call my dad.

"Those are high," he says and has us take another reading with me lying down. The numbers aren't as high, but still above normal, per my dad. I type them into my Notes app, too. It's all a bit over my head at this point.

"Every few hours, take another read. If the numbers go up again, call your doctor right away," my dad advises. "Just stay in bed, resting, until your appointment tomorrow."

I do, and the numbers stay the same.

When I arrive at my appointment, I feel relieved to see Susan, the nurse who has been taking care of me at each visit. We'd bonded early on because she, too, had my doctor for her pregnancies years ago and mentioned this doc is the one trusted by all the nurses for their babies—that she could do a delivery "with her eyes closed," she is that good. I tell her about my high blood pressure, and she hands me a cup to pee in.

When the urine test comes back a few minutes later, Susan tells me it has protein in it.

She walks me over to an empty patient bay.

"When do you next see your doctor?" she asks while hooking me up to the fetal heart monitor.

"Just after this," I say, getting settled on my side.

"I'm going to give her a call. I think she'll want you to go directly to the hospital instead. Your delivery might be sooner than you think."

"Oh, okay." I nod, knowing I was going somewhere after this anyway and to change course doesn't feel like too big a deal. I have a bag with hospital essentials tucked away in the trunk of our car; the crib is up, we have diapers, and while my sister was here, she helped me install my niece and nephew's old car seat. I'm ready.

Susan wraps an automatic blood pressure cuff around my arm and fastens a strap around my belly, then steps away.

I sit—on my own—feeling the cuff inflate, while staring at the zigzagged lines printing out of the machine in front of me.

When Susan is back at my side, she unstraps the cuff first.

"Yeah, those numbers are high."

Not something I don't know, I think, expecting as much and grateful I'm here, in her care.

She then steps over to the long piece of paper, continuing to pile up on the floor. She goes through the folds, pulling a few of them flat to study the zigzags.

"There are a few inconsistencies here," she says, drawing my attention more to the horizontal sections and sharp valleys than the peaks. "We're unable to detect the baby's heartbeat with any sort of regularity and don't like seeing these dips. There aren't too many—but they are here," she says and points at the paper, pulling it toward me, "and there."

What? Dips? Irregular heartbeat? I think, sensing something more serious going on than just my high blood pressure.

I look over to Susan, but she is calm.

"Your doctor and I agree: Hospital triage is your next stop."

"And you think it's okay for me to drive myself over there?" I ask, feeling out how scared I need to be here.

"I do."

"Okay, thank you."

She unbuckles my belly from the machine, and I move off

the bed to tug on my jacket. Before heading back to her desk, Susan holds me in a brief hug.

The triage nurse repeats the urine test (it also shows protein), takes my blood pressure (still high), and then hooks me up to the fetal monitor (noting, too, some dips in the baby's heartbeat).

I hold my breath each time the baby's heartbeat is undetectable by the belt that is again wrapped around my abdomen, and I release it each time a new spike appears on the recorded tracings that spit out of the machine and collect in a new pool of paper.

There is urgency, but still no panic. I have blood drawn and am admitted; the room doesn't feel like the main event, but a holding space. Mark makes it to my side by the time the on-call doctor checks in.

"You have preeclampsia," the doctor begins, "and we just received your blood test results. They show that you also have HELLP syndrome…"

Help? What the heck is that? Yes, I need help, I think and chuckle to myself, not grasping the gravity of the situation.

"So right now," the doctor continues, "I have two patients. You and the baby."

Oh. That sounds more alarming.

"We will not be letting you go home until the baby is safely out. If things stay the same, we'll keep him in as long as possible, considering you are just shy of thirty-six weeks. If things change or get worse, we'll look at inducing you."

I nod, staring now so I don't miss any details.

"You might be here for a few weeks or a few days. It's hard to tell. But, husband—" He turns to Mark. "I'd advise you go home and get some rest for the night."

I don't know what HELLP syndrome is other than

something wonky with my blood count that has developed because of preeclampsia. I later learn that I have a low platelet count, elevated liver enzymes, and my red blood cells are breaking down. Lots of things could go wrong: My liver could rupture, my kidneys could fail, I could have a stroke. And I could die. But in this moment, I am just grateful to be at the hospital in capable hands for these Greek-to-me complications, mostly in an ignorance-is-bliss state.

The alarm hasn't registered. Maybe they never really wanted it to register so I would remain calm.

I'm given blood pressure medication and deemed stable in light of my new diagnoses. Mark heads home to feed the cat, shower, and get some shut-eye. I settle into my hospital bed for the night, pull out my headphones from the bag I stashed away in the car, and start season five of *Downton Abbey* on my iPhone. *The perfect time!* I think, smiling to myself as the familiar theme begins behind the opening credits. I'm instantly warmed by the characters I'd been waiting until my maternity leave to watch.

The fetal monitor is still plugged in and strapped onto my belly, but the sound is switched off. I soon drift in and out of sleep as the nurses check my vitals every few hours and review the long receipt-like trail of heartbeats that keeps inching out.

20 | a swell of warmth

The next morning, Mark arrives just before 9:00 a.m., showered and fresh. The sun is out and the Northern California winter light pushes in past the curtains, landing on the blond wood–like floor of my room. Neither of us got a whole lot of sleep last night—me, from the constant monitoring, and him, from worrying about a big meeting tomorrow he'll likely have to miss—but we're both ready to see what the day will bring, surrendering to the help of the hospital.

Within minutes, a new doctor knocks on my door, alert and purposeful, just starting his rounds. He is older, definitely more senior staff, with a couple of nurses flanking his sides.

He walks into the room looking from his clipboard and up to me. "Is this the same person?" he asks, as if I'm not sitting right in front of him.

He flips the page around to show Mark the copy of my driver's license photo he has, which must be from my registration records. *Kind of weird*, I think as I plaster on a smile. I'm not *that* much of a balloon, am I?

He introduces himself, then quickly gets to the point. "I spoke with the on-call doctor in your practice, who's been in touch with your doctor, okay?"

"Okay…"

"And we're all in agreement that we're going to start the labor induction process today."

That is quite a shift from yesterday's unknown timing. "How come?"

"You're a lot worse off than the doctors let on last night and let me just say, I'm glad you're here."

He explains that the primary treatment for HELLP syndrome is delivery of the baby and that my life and the baby's are at risk if we delay.

I feel oddly casual in response, more bummed that my *Downton Abbey* marathon has been cut short than having any anxiety that I could die. In fact, death never penetrates my consciousness as a real possibility, even as this doctor assures us that it is, because I feel like it's their job to worry, not mine. My job is being here, and I've done that.

Not much else I can do other than follow orders.

"We're going to move you a floor up," the doctor says. "Give us about an hour, and once you're settled in with the Labor and Delivery team, we'll start you on a medicine similar to Pitocin."

The nurses wheel out the breakfast tray and unhook the monitors. I feel very relaxed watching them pulled from the room, with my still-high blood pressure, still-proteined urine, and puffy face. Must be the pills they've given me.

"Once she gets Pitocin, how long does it take for labor to begin?" Mark asks, not having any medicine on board, his anxiety increasing.

"It's hard to know exactly," the doctor says, then turns to me. "We'll give you an oral pill every twelve hours to see if you start dilating. It may take a day or two."

He nods and leaves, along with the nurses.

Mark and I have the space to ourselves.

"A day or two doesn't sound that bad," I say, moving my legs off the bed. "I'm going to shower."

Mark ducks out to grab us another set of clothes from home, the matching newborn onesie and hat I set aside for the baby's arrival, and a couple of our favorite green smoothies with banana and ginger from our neighborhood coffee shop.

When he returns, I'm in the new room. My window is behind the tuft of a Brisbane box tree and gives me a glimpse of the pedestrians and buses passing back and forth on the street below.

The room has a sink along the back wall, multiple drawers, and scientific-looking instruments reminiscent of my high school chemistry lab. This birthing suite is ready for action. But last the nurse checked, my body is not.

That evening, Mark catches up with work on his laptop, trying to get comfortable in a visitor sleeper chair. I lie patiently across from him after taking my second Pitocin-like pill.

"Do you think we can order dinner?" I ask Shirley, who says she'll be my nurse for the night. She shares my paternal grandmother's name, which I find quite special and easy to remember.

"Sure, hon, this usually takes a while," she says, handing us a menu.

Around 8:30 p.m., we both finish our food and turn out the lights. The sun set long ago. We text our families that not much has changed, and I fall asleep to the glow of Mark's computer illuminating his face in concentration, next to him on his now-converted bed.

I wake to the sensation of something wet leaking out of me. I pop up in the dark. The clock reads 12:30 a.m.

"Mark!" I say, trying to wake him. "Mark!"

"What? What? I'm up," he says.

"I think my water just broke!" I announce. Maybe things are moving along quicker than we thought they would. "I'm just going to stand up to see." I push a button to turn on the lamp attached to my bed and slide off, steadying my feet on the vinyl flooring. I lift up my gown to look at my leg. The liquid trickling down is not clear. It is bright red.

"Oh, that's blood." My heartbeat rises as if I've seen an animal in the forest that might be coming for me. I'm not sure.

Mark doesn't skip a beat. "I'll go find a nurse," he says and heads out of the room in his pajamas. I push the call button as well.

Shirley hurries back in with Mark.

"That is not your water breaking, sweetie, but could be an indication of something else going on." She speaks kindly but moves quickly, getting me back onto the bed. "Let me go get the on-call doctor. Sit tight."

I suddenly feel very young and vulnerable.

Within minutes, Shirley reappears with a doctor who moves to the latest collection of printed paper and points to more dips in the baby's heartbeat.

"This," the doctor says, "along with the blood, could be an indication of placenta previa." She catches my eye in the lone beam of light coming off the bed lamp. "That means the placenta is starting to detach, and we'll need to go in right away to make sure the baby is safe."

"Yikes," I say, frozen in time.

"We're going to get the hospital's obstetrician in here and call the on-call doctor from your practice," she explains. "Meanwhile, Shirley," she says and turns, "please prep her for the OR."

There is a lot of movement around me.

Good thing I'm already in a surgical gown, I think. *Not so nice that I ate dinner.*

The hospital's OB enters a few minutes later and explains, as calmly as possible, that they're going to perform an emergency C-section to get the baby out now. In a way, I'm grateful this is the middle of the night and I still feel half asleep—or maybe it's the medicine I'm on?—because the adrenaline isn't reaching me like it is for everyone else.

I'm handed some documents to sign, given a surgical cap to cover my hair, and my bed is wheeled into an operating room. I lose sight of Mark, but Shirley assures me they'll take care of him and bring him in when it's time.

He later tells me that, during the twenty tortuous minutes he was left behind, he called our parents, keeping everyone in Colorado and South Africa in the loop and awake with tense anticipation.

My contacts are already out since I've been sleeping, but I have my glasses on this time. I try not to look at all the glistening sterile utensils too closely. Shirley walks me through receiving an epidural. She rubs my back to steady my breathing as my nerves threaten to skyrocket, thinking of a needle near my spinal cord.

I hardly feel the jab before my legs go numb.

Just then an OB from my doctor's practice steps into the OR. This is our first time meeting, and I like her instantly. She is bright-eyed and polished for one in the morning, with a shiny red patent-leather Louis Vuitton purse secured purposefully under her arm.

"How did you get here so fast?" I ask.

"I just live around the corner in Russian Hill," she explains and goes on to cheerily tell me about her life and children as if the time is really just two o'clock in the afternoon. Her easy chatter and impressive demeanor calm me.

Shirley lowers my body down on the bed. A blue tarp is erected from my waist to the ceiling to block my view of the commencing surgical activity. Music is turned on in the background. The vibe is happy and lively. A swell of warmth appears within me.

The anesthesiologist is at my side, getting an IV set up. Mark is now in the room with me, too, holding my other hand.

The surgery begins. There is some rummaging around that I am only vaguely aware of thanks to the medicinal magic disconnecting me from any pain.

"Things are looking good," the doctor informs us. "We're about to pull out the baby."

Leonard Cohen's "Hallelujah"—a favorite ballad of Mark's and mine—plays.

I whisper to Mark that this is so well-orchestrated, recalling all the pressures for a "birth plan" from peers and media that felt so superfluous to me. Those sorts of wishes felt like excessive cherries on top that I didn't want to stop and warrant. And I'm glad I didn't take on the pressure to make something up and demand it anyway—because releasing myself into the hands around me feels better than I could've ever imagined.

"Here he is!" the doc says, and we hear our son's little baby wail. "He looks great."

Tears I didn't know I'd been holding in finally spill out in elation. Mark squeezes my hand.

The baby is okay, I am okay. We are safe.

"Aha! There is the placenta detaching, I see," the doctor says. "It's a good thing we got him out when we did!"

A nurse takes the baby to be washed, weighed, and swaddled, calling Mark over to cut the umbilical cord. Being just over six pounds and arriving at thirty-six weeks exactly, we are told he does not need to go to the neonatal intensive care unit.

I am relieved, but as the doctor stitches me up, I feel nauseous from the pressure on my stomach.

"Oh no," I say. "I'm going to throw up."

"Not to worry," the anesthesiologist says and moves a bean-shaped pan next to me.

I turn my head and a yellow liquid spurts out of my mouth, one heave after another.

I am so drained when it's over but stay awake and smile because Mark is bringing our little boy over. We kiss his cheek and name him Gideon.

My inability to breastfeed (because I do not *have* any breast tissue) turns out to be a blessing in disguise. Even though it is surely written on my chart and frustrating to have to repeat numerous times during my stay, it also means that Gideon can stay overnight in the hospital nursery so I can sink into sleep.

The following morning, I find such pleasure in my steaming cup of black coffee, along with a rich slice of chocolate cake from the hospital menu, that months later, in the throes of night feeds, baby gassiness, and my own sleep deprivation, I will daydream of returning to this exact moment of indulgence and support.

21 | melting and reshaping

I mogen, parenting is hard. Adjusting to life with a newborn is even more full-on than we could've ever imagined. As two very high-functioning adults, your father and I are surprised to feel on the back foot in regard to just about everything.

We quickly become "shushing" machines. SIDS (sudden infant death syndrome), which the doctors drill into us—at the hospital and subsequent pediatric appointments—keeps us excessively vigilant. We eat all of our meals with our plates in our laps, on the floor by Gideon's crib to decipher his noises and make sure our cat doesn't jump in and accidentally suffocate him. We try to laugh it off and tell our friends we're in the "baby cave," but at the same time, we become increasingly apprehensive whenever we leave our post.

The hardest part, though, is recalibrating my mind from the ease I assumed would click into place with parenting to the reality of constant problem-solving in areas completely foreign to me. I skim through books left and right to take in the highlighted advice, make notes on my phone, and log what is and isn't working in notebooks I leave all over the house. I have Mad Hatter energy, trying to compile an all-in-one manual of sorts for my baby that I am unable to find elsewhere. I have a fierce love for my firstborn, yet a complete loss of confidence at the same time. Imogen, it is all trial and error.

Simultaneously, I am trying to come to terms with how consuming this new role is and that there isn't a place for me at my old job, where I actually know what I am doing. My request to work part-time isn't accommodated, and no other part-time positions beckon me.

To combat this helplessness, this overwhelm, I keep returning to our desire: to raise our children ourselves rather than vet a stranger to fill in for us. I take happy pictures in moments of peace—first smiles, first frowns, funny happenings in-between. Being the one to capture them centers me.

On our first trip with Gideon to Colorado that summer, I sit with my mom on her wide porch swing and admire the draping wisteria that only blooms for a few rare weeks. I can see the Continental Divide mountain range in the distance, its peaks snow-free and dry, and envy it standing there so solidly as the sun beats down.

I, on the other hand, feel like I'm constantly melting and reshaping every day, unable to find one form that fits in a marathon of thrown-into-the-deep-end kind of reactive learning.

"I don't know if I want to be pregnant again," I confess. "We had a positive outcome, thank goodness—but going through it all was a lot. So is this adjustment to parenting."

Truthfully, I'd forgotten this, Imogen. It is easy to forget the hard times when you get through them to the easy times. Maybe we want to forget them.

"Parenting is the hardest thing you'll ever do," my mother replies.

"Thanks, Mom," I say, somewhat flatly. She's stating the

obvious. And hearing it doesn't make this longer-than-expected transition any easier. I know she knows but that she has forgotten, too.

"You don't have to make a decision now," she reminds me.

We rock back and forth as I breathe, still trying to catch up with this seismic shift in my life.

I nod to myself, *Yes, I don't have to make a decision now*, while mentally recalling my doctors' guidance that I'll need at least two years between transfers anyway. That is a good amount of daylight.

Mid-2016, when Gideon is almost a year and a half old, I feel like I've got a miraculously good routine going at home.

I'm through it—what feels like the hard yards of learning something new. I've created my own baby manual, a guide for me of all the things to remember with a new baby, all the helpful resources to grab in a pinch. With the hope that it could be a much-needed tool for others as well, I design, print, and publish my compilation. I feel on top of things. On top of something. Myself and my well-being most of all.

It is in this creative, confident space—*my* space, finally—that I come around. Grateful for the forced two-year interval between transfers, I welcome the steps to become pregnant again with our second male embryo. The schedule, and even the administering of different injections, is familiar and easy to follow. Underneath it all still lies an invisible barrier between me and another pregnancy—the IVF hoops that I must summon the willpower to go through again—but I don't second-guess my decision. I am ready.

My second pregnancy is less marked in time by every scan or

appointment and more by the changes happening outside of my body.

We do the big Bay Area thing of touring preschools and juggling childcare to pitch up to the required open days and presentations of the one we want to be in the most, kid-free. We move to the apartment above us in our same building, for the extra bedroom. Our octogenarian landlord moves into our old spot, and we adjust to the ins and outs of renovations happening to accommodate her arrival.

One winter's day, after refinishing the floorboards of our old place, the handyman leaves the windows closed and varnish fumes waft upward. The strong smell—on top of a long day of walking the hills of San Francisco and pushing a full stroller without drinking enough water—triggers debilitating cramps in my abdomen. I am thirty-three weeks along.

By the evening, unable to sit comfortably, much less lie down, I duck into an Uber and head to the hospital triage. Mark stays home with Gideon, who is already asleep for the night.

Once I hear from the nurse that my baby's activity is okay and my blood pressure is normal, I see a male on-call obstetrician.

"You are having early onset contractions," he says, "which are more painful than regular contractions."

How the hell does he know?! I wonder grumpily, in pain.

"We're going to keep you in for monitoring…"

I hardly hear him. I just want the pain to stop.

"Given your history with your first pregnancy, we want to make sure nothing else is going on."

I wrap my arms around my waist, supporting myself on my side. "Why do you think I'm having these contractions?" I grumble.

"It could be stress or dehydration."

Given my day, both of those sound likely.

Sweet relief only comes hours later. I'm admitted overnight, and at 3:00 a.m., after extensive whining, a nurse gives me morphine. I finally get some rest. Around 9:00 a.m., I am discharged with a regimen of calcium-channel blockers to stop the preterm contractions for the next ten days.

Ten days later, I'm back in triage with contractions and no dilation.

"We are worried that you'll have a placental abruption again or some repeat performance of last time," the on-call doctor says, "so we'd like to go ahead and do a C-section. Tonight."

This doesn't send me awash in worry but rather keeps me coasting at neutral. Perhaps because of the emergency delivery I had with Gideon that I don't wish to repeat, if possible. Looking at the facts, I am a little over thirty-five weeks and do not have high blood pressure (yet?). The contractions are painful, and I'm not in love with the idea of having them remain for the next few weeks or having to return daily in worry for monitoring. Nor do I know how much more ambiguity I can handle in terms of the baby's (or my!) well-being.

Having the opportunity to come to this conclusion midday in a rational way feels refreshingly civilized.

My dad, now in town, is also in agreement.

"Let's do it," I say. "One more thing, though? My doc and I planned to have my fallopian tubes removed if I had another C-section. So, considering that is the case today, I want to be sure it's done."

My oncologist and obstetrician confirmed that this would be the next best step for me in regard to ovarian cancer prevention with my BRCA1 gene. If for some reason I wanted or needed to do another round of IVF and retrieve eggs, I still could without my fallopian tubes. And, if I wanted to transfer another embryo, I could still get pregnant and carry a baby because my uterus would remain intact. This felt like minimal risk with the upside of built-in contraception, making the addition of any future children a very thought-out and deliberate decision.

"Oh, yes, I see that request here," she says a minute later. "Both sides, correct? So, a bilateral salpingectomy?"

I raise my eyebrows, uncertain of the lingo, and glance over at my dad. He nods.

"Yes."

"Great, we have you scheduled for 6:00 p.m. I'm still on call then, so will be doing your delivery. We'll get you upstairs to be prepped."

Imogen, your youngest brother is born to Bruce Springsteen's "I'm on Fire"—another classic we enjoy that came on in the background, unplanned. We smile, making a note of it as possible foreshadowing of his personality, and name him Julian.

When he is wrapped and placed in my arms, Leonard Cohen's ballad "Dance Me to the End of Love" plays, making me think of Mila and the dance parties we had at her home before kids, under a full moon. Its haunting melody elicits a connection in me to all facets of us—before now, now, and whatever may come next.

A month or two after Julian turns a year old, I am itching to get back to work, feeling it is time. Time to fill a part of me again that is separate from parenting. The part that is productive beyond the confines of home. A part that would like to reengage in collaboration with other professionals.

There must be a way to make it work without compromising our goals, I think, seeing numerous others doing the same. Wondering if maybe our goals are shifting. If *my* goals are shifting.

I call the supervisor at the construction company that previously employed me, expressing my drive to make time for a project in a supportive capacity, seeing if something has come up that needs an extra hand. Surely, there is something I can do. Purchase orders, perhaps? Transcribing pink sheets into budgets? A few design sketches for a client, even? Yes, please, that would be so much fun!

"Okay, let me think about it," he says in response—never to be in touch with me again.

Fuck.

Even so, making space for work becomes my mission.

I find a day care for Julian three mornings a week, and things fall into place pretty easily after that. I get an easy yes to work part-time with my previous, female, interior design boss in the city. She has two boys of her own and is used to straddling schedules to make it all work.

I plan to see her and the team in person two mornings a week, to help with her new start-up. The remaining morning of day care will allow me to tackle anything and everything around the house—that there never feels like enough time to do—kid-free. It's a gift of a schedule, and I love it all.

I love seeing my old boss's new office in a shared workspace and being among the focus there. I love being welcomed back into the fold like no time has passed and I don't have to explain away my absence or prove myself. I love being able to vacuum, do laundry, and prep meals with no other on-the-spot demands.

Let's just say, though, that life had other plans in mind that my determination could not match.

My unreliability begins with a bout of conjunctivitis from day care. Both of Julian's eyes get infected, so he stays home for twenty-four hours after his first antibiotic drops. Then, my eyes get infected—so, same. And, sure enough, Gideon's eyes get infected, too, and he has to stay home. There go two weeks of in-person meetings or follow-ups due to not wanting to pass on pink, goopy eyes.

The following week, Julian throws up in the car on the way to day care. Is it a bug or carsickness? Day care isn't about to find out, so home we go. When we get there, he projectile vomits across the living room.

Great. My body slinks as I set him in a playpen so I can clean up the mess without him getting into it. *Now Julian will be home again for a few days,* I think, scrubbing the carpet, *which means I will be, too.*

Gideon then rides a fighting-illness frenzy that culminates into a scary-for-me febrile seizure. He picks up different viruses left and right from either his classroom or his brother—being, for the first time, on antibiotics more often than not.

We get through it, but the hits of unexpected needs keep coming until I am only able to release control over my separate-seeming work life with a note of hilarity.

I'm unable to do both simultaneously with any sense of pride or purpose. So, I come to terms with my children still needing a constant presence at home—and that presence, for us, being a parent (me) and not a nanny.

My boss, kindly and graciously, understands and we part with nothing but warm feelings. It seems our goals are still as they were, but my inner, before-kids Lindsay really appreciates being remembered—even if it was for just a hot second.

By the fall of 2018, both of the boys are in school and for more hours in the week. I fill my time volunteering in their school's admissions office and speaking to new families on the open day tours. I befriend other parents in the community and also take homeopathy classes at our pediatrician's office. They're a lot of fun and help me curb the boys' coughs and mood swings with different remedies.

But both endeavors feel more temporary than indicative of any future career paths.

I keep being pulled back to the question, *What is next?*

And in pondering the answer, I keep being pulled further back, to the first week after we brought Julian home from the hospital.

One morning, I stayed in bed with him while my mom took Gideon out adventuring. Mark was on paternity leave, responding to emails in the other room, and as I rocked Julian to sleep, a maternal wave of peace rolled over me. *I could have a third,* I thought. Then I perked up, looked side to side, and wondered,

Wait. Where did that come from?

When Mark joined me a few minutes later, I couldn't help but share with him. "I just had this big feeling of calm with the idea of a third. Funny, as I wasn't expecting that. Maybe it's because of our other embryo?"

"Must be your hormones talking." He laughed and sat down on the bed next to us. He tugged Julian's hat back on, as it had slipped off and bunched behind his head.

"Ha! Probably! But seriously, I needed to say it out loud because I'm so startled by the feeling!"

He looked at me and smiled. "I kind of feel that way, too, if I'm honest."

"Really?!" I said, a twinkle in my eye. "Strange, hey?"

"Mmmhmm," he said, hanging onto the idea with me.

"I guess I'm just enjoying the fact that some unknown door seems to have unlocked, showing me that I could handle it."

"I hear you." He audibly inhaled. "But let's just take things one day at a time."

"Of course. I'm not actually saying I want a third and let's plan on it. It's just interesting that this feeling appeared."

Maybe it was because my mom was there helping. Maybe it was because Mark was around, too, and I didn't feel alone handling it all. Maybe it was because the recovery was quicker and I knew a little more of how to meet Julian's needs. But more—all of a sudden—felt doable.

Like it does again now with this extra space arriving around me.

In October, the loss of Mark's gran at one hundred years old becomes the excuse I need to really shine a light on these feelings. I ask Mark, when he returns home from her memorial service in South Africa, "What if we have this third embryo and give her your grandmother's name? Or use it for her middle name?"

Her name is Louise. The name Imogen comes later, when you're closer to being with us, because we keep imagining you here and the name sounds like "im-a-gin." *Imagine.* It also mimics the number of syllables in your brothers' names.

"But what about the BRCA gene?" Mark asks, steadying me, trying to keep me from going too far down this road.

"I keep thinking about it and wondering, is it *really* a nonstarter? What if she never gets cancer? We don't know…"

"I know, but what if she *does*? Do we want to bring her into this world knowing she has a *significantly* increased chance of getting cancer than her non-BRCA-carrying peers?" he retorts. "Or that she is nearly 100 percent likely to need preventative surgeries? I thought we made this decision already, Lindsay."

His words hang in the air with an emphasis, like, *Hel-lo? Are you in there?*

I am impressed with Mark's ability to retain facts and lock the information into his brain that mothering hormones have somehow wiped from mine. He does this with the names of my cousins and their children that I told him once, years ago. It is a superpower I do not have. My memory has also blocked out all the other tough stuff, like birth complications and IVF worries— even my experience with cancer. It all feels so far away now.

Gosh, maybe I do have blinders on, I think. *Do I need to take them off?*

"I don't know," I admit, my energy flattened.

23 | truth

I haven't seen the shaman in a while and set up an appointment to discuss my newly brewing quandary.

"I'm really feeling pulled to this other embryo," I tell him. "And not just any embryo—the one we have, in waiting."

He listens as I continue.

"The boys are so wonderful—and so wild—it's like I feel they could use a sister to care for, to balance them out. Much like Mark and his brothers with their younger sister," I add.

"Mmm."

"And! It's like Mark's gran wants to return; she never did want to let go and held on for so long. Could this child be asking us to come, through her energy almost? Is that possible?"

Can he sense these things? How cool would that be if he knew! Can he channel your voice? I start to wonder.

"What do *you* want, Lindsay?" His question stops my rambling chatter. "This isn't about what his gran may or may not want. Don't let that sway you."

Dang. Is this me trying to hand over control in favor of connection, or is this me needing to break an old habit *again*—so that I may re-ground myself in my own voice?

I breathe and try to wipe away the noise.

"I want to want it," I say. "Because she is like me, you know? And I'm grateful for my life. I want to be here and am happy with my choices, even though the moments up until now have been hard…" I pause. "I feel like she would be grateful for her life, too…but I don't know."

"I understand that. It is a hard place to be in. A hard decision to sit with."

And I wait for it. Wait for him to let me in on some upper world revelation saying I must go one way or another. Yet, like last time, with whether or not to have my reconstructive surgery, the shaman makes no decision for me and my conundrum remains my own.

"Something I do, that might help you," he offers, "is talking aloud to myself. In the shower or at bedtime. Quietly."

"Really? How does that help?"

"You'll see. You can work through things. Speech is sacred, and through this vessel the upper world can appear in your words to yourself. Try it."

"Okay. I'll try it."

I don't see the shaman again for a long time, but I do this practice off and on. Mostly in the car on my way to pick up the boys from school. It feels less silly than when I'm in the shower or whispering to myself at bedtime with Mark nearby. But the more I process my thoughts out loud, the more I find answers—or the confidence to uncover them.

I speak to the boys' pediatrician, also a mother at their school and someone I've come to love and trust, about our third embryo. She refers me to a gynecologist in Marin that a friend of hers with a similar history to mine sees and adores.

A week later, when I walk into this new-to-me doctor's

lobby, I immediately see another parent from the boys' school who I recently met and admire. She walks over to greet me with a tight hug. Her long straight chestnut hair flaps on her back as she pulls away.

"So lovely to run into you!" she says, her arms on my shoulders. "I'm pregnant with my third."

"Oh, congratulations!" I say. Her brightness is infectious.

Was that a sign? I wonder when I'm called to an exam room.

The doctor is about my age with dark curly hair and a smile nearly as warm as the mom's from the reception area. She immediately engages with me in a way that feels like an ally. I don't feel judged—like another doctor I tried to see who told me it was imperative I go back to work, without hearing my experience or opinion—so am very relaxed as we review my history.

"What do you think about me having this female embryo with the BRCA1 gene?" I ask. "I feel crazy to consider it."

"First of all, I don't think you are crazy," she says, "as this is a very normal question. I am supportive of whatever you decide…"

Oooh, I like her more already. I lean forward as excitement brews in me that this could be a real possibility.

"And something I'd like you to consider, shall you proceed, is that she will have different options and better support than you ever did as a carrier of this gene."

Oh, gosh.

"You really think so?"

"Well, we are learning so much about BRCA every day. It is very well-funded in its research. We know more now than ever before and will continue to progress in that knowledge and data. Truthfully, we can't even know what her future will look like in twenty years when she'd be faced with the decision of prophylactic surgery."

Goose bumps dot my skin as I let that idea sink in.

"So, when making your decision, just know it doesn't need to be entirely based on your experience ten years ago because already—today—we know more about this gene than we did then."

I nod and bite a dry piece of skin at my cuticle—my most frequent tell that I'm thinking.

"I would also like to add that you are still in your early thirties. You are healthy. You are capable. There isn't anything, to me, screaming that your body wouldn't be able to handle another pregnancy or even be able to try a VBAC if you wanted to go that route."

A vaginal birth after having undergone two C-sections? That definitely wasn't on my bingo card, nor was I expecting this unabashed vote of confidence. It is almost too much to handle—adding more into my cart than I'd bargained for—but I walk away feeling a rainbow of potential around the idea of transferring our BRCA1 embryo, having found a doctor advocating for me in this way.

Maybe our thinking around having this embryo has been too doomsday?

I call Mark on my drive home. He steps out of a meeting to hear uninhibited enthusiasm tumble from my lips.

"Okay, okay, I'm listening," he says. I can almost picture him raising a hand to pause me. "Let's talk about it more when I get home."

Later, we do, and I am still unable to land on a certain yes or no in the face of his doubts. The weight of remembering what I've been through keeps me from leaping forward, especially in front of Mark, who's been a steady witness to the ups and downs.

But the more we debate, the more rooted I feel in a

newfound power that is flushing into me, like my insides are expanding to this possibility of a yes.

A couple of days later, I am having coffee with a new mom friend of mine from the boys' school. These moms are really propelling me, like examples of super people who can do it all. The more time I spend with them, the more capable I feel.

Funny how being in their ether works—but also funny is that there is a lot I don't see, like how much support they have behind the scenes or what they struggle with. Nonetheless, I love the confidence and joy that radiates out of them and being swept up in their orbit.

We find a table for two with our fancy mint-laden brews from Philz Coffee in Corte Madera. Somehow, this mom settles in quickly, picking up right where we left off on a hike a few weeks ago where I told her about my journey with cancer, of having the BRCA gene, and of you, Imogen.

"If you could do *anything* right now, at this moment," she asks, "what would it be?"

She leans in, patient, still.

And I am not. The answer bursts out of me. Almost like it has been waiting all this time for permission—from someone, anyone—to just ask, point-blank, no-holds-barred, as she has. "I'd have a third child." I pause. "I'd have *this* child, the one I know is waiting for me—and is just like me."

Uh, whoa. I lean back in shock. That was a big revelation to a near stranger. I start second-guessing myself right after the words leave my lips. But at the same time, feel invincible and free.

"I can feel your clarity." Her eyes glow, matching the glow in mine. "I say, go for it! What is stopping you?"

"Thank you," I sigh, then answer plainly: "Fear. It is all fear."

And my legs turn to jelly at the admission.

24 | poking

After coffee, I, of course, call Mark.

"My truth has declared itself!" I say. "I want this. I want her. I'm ready to move forward."

I am on a high. Back to that elation post-chemo, where anything is possible and a resounding *Why sweat the small stuff?* sweeps through me. Life is grand. Life is mysterious. Life is full of infinite potential. *Is Mark feeling what I'm feeling?* I chew at my nails.

"Okay," he says.

"Okay?" I ask, not wanting to mistake what he is okay-ing.

"Let's do this. I am ready, too."

"Really? Yay! Okay!"

We enter happy-tears territory together. This yes feels like the greatest gift.

It's the spring of 2019 and after years of feeling like I've been treading water, unable to move forward, I finally have a launching pad.

As soon as I get home, I call my IVF doctor's office, like there is no time to waste. From the kitchen, I stare out at the blooming jasmine cascading down our fence. *How did now arrive so soon?* I laugh, realizing that Julian just turned two and, again, I've found my feet as a parent, ready for my next marching orders. The maturation feels good and abundant like those delicate petals forming hundreds of stars winking at me through the window.

I get through to the receptionist and while she checks my doc's schedule, I visualize her declaring an opening later in the week, or something next week.

"We're really booked out right now," she says, "but I can get you in for an appointment the morning of June tenth."

Shit. That is a couple of months away. The week before summer break. My fingers are cold, and I sit on them as I press her for something sooner.

"Isn't there a cancellation list you could put me on?"

Surely something will open up, my mind encourages me.

"I can put you on a list, but it is unlikely," she says. "Would you like the tenth?"

Her tone indicates she doesn't have time to get my hopes up. That she has other patients who would happily snag this appointment, if it isn't me.

"Okay." I sigh. "Please put me down for the tenth."

I hang up, and a sadness swells in me—a quicksand that is eager to lap me back up into limbo, just below this newfound solidity.

Stay in it, Lindsay, I tell myself. *Stay in the happiness you have. Don't let this later appointment date take that away.*

My heart races as I think of the next thing I know I need to do now that this decision has been made. Something that could negate the disappointment of a delayed doctor appointment and still make this feel real: tell my dad.

I will myself to return to my earlier wave of enthusiasm, pick the phone back up, and call him. Unable to remain still, I stand up and walk down the hall.

"Hey Beetle," he says. "What's up?"

"Hey, Dad, I have some news I want to share with you." *Oof, this feels loaded and ominous already. What was I thinking? What is he thinking?*

"Okay, shoot."

Just push through, Lindsay, I tell myself. *No one said this would be easy, and this is what you want. Own it.*

"Well," I say and take a deep breath, "Mark and I have decided that we are going to go ahead and transfer our BRCA1 female embryo."

"Oh, okay." He waits a beat. "That's a big thing."

"We've given it a lot of thought and we're ready. It is what we both want."

I feel like a little girl again, looking up to my father for his approval. I know he sees us as equals, so why does my inner world instantly go there? I sink my toes into the carpet of our bedroom floor and look out at our backyard oak tree to brace myself for whatever is coming. I slowly exhale.

"Well, if you don't mind my asking, how come this embryo? If you'd really like a third child, wouldn't you want to try another round of IVF for an embryo that doesn't carry the gene?"

"Good question." I inhale deeply. His tone is supportive. "We've thought about that. But, no." I exhale. "This is the one we want and why we're saying yes. I don't really want to go through IVF again when we have this otherwise healthy embryo. She is like me and I feel like that is important..."

I breathe again. *You've got this, Lindsay.*

"And," I add, "I know you weren't given the choice, but I'd rather be here than not, and that is what I'm feeling from this embryo, too."

I sit down as my emotions bang around the surface. I love my dad so much and have never liked that he feels responsible for my experiences. They are out of his control, and if I could take away the guilt he feels, I would.

I cross and recross my legs, bobbing my foot up and down.

"Okay, sweetie. If you feel good about it, then I am happy for you and here for you."

I know that was difficult for him to say, and I appreciate it so much. I let my breath out.

My mom, who must've been listening in the background, intercepts the call. "We are here for you and support you, honey," she says.

"Thank you."

"But just know that patients of ours, too, have had a hard time with their frozen embryos and knowing whether or not to use them."

Instantly, I feel discounted. She hasn't been in my shoes.

"Just because you have the embryo doesn't mean you have to use it," she adds.

I stand up again and pace to diffuse the fury igniting in me. Even though I know she is trying to help, she doesn't have BRCA1. She has never gone through IVF. She doesn't have any frozen embryos, healthy or not, and I don't want her opinion.

"I get it, Mom," I say. "As I told Dad, we've given this a lot of thought." And I can't help it, but my voice rises. "It's not like we're making an off-the-cuff decision here."

"Okay, I just want to make sure…" she starts, and I cut her off. I've shared my truth and don't want it poked at.

"Thank you. We're not giving in to fear, okay? We're moving forward with this."

"Okay, sweetie," she says, stopping herself from any further proclamations. "We love you and are here for you."

"Great, thank you," I bark out. I add an "I love you, too," then hang up. I throw myself on the bed and bury my face in my pillows as the built-up feelings release in guttural sobs.

I just want so much to have this baby and be supported.

So much more than I realized.

That evening, Gideon is practicing spelling his classmates' names with a bath crayon on the tub walls while Julian, mid-potty training, is running around naked in pure bliss after a nap.

"What is Grandpa's job?" Gideon suddenly asks, looking up at me.

"Oh, Colorado Grandpa?"

"Yeah."

I pause, wondering how best to reply. "He helps babies come into the world."

"How?"

"He is a doctor."

"That is what I want to do when I grow up."

"You want to be a doctor that helps bring babies into the world?"

"Yeah."

I haven't heard this from him before, but go with it, wondering if there is something else he is trying to get at. He turns his gaze back to the red crayon leaving a trail of letters on the shiny enamel, then looks up at me again.

"When are we going to have another baby?"

Ah, there it is.

"Because I'd like to have a sister," he says.

"Well…" I say, buying time. *Do I tell him? Do I not tell him? What do I tell him?* It is hard to skirt around a question when a child asks you directly.

Since we have decided to move forward, I feel like this is the universe testing me again. Testing me again, so soon—to see if we are ready.

So, I tell him.

"We are going to try and have another baby. Hopefully a sister for you. We'll see how it goes…" Then I add, "I'm actually going to meet with a doctor in a couple of months to help start the process."

When he doesn't respond, I let it go, just as he seems to have, now drawing little figures next to the names he has written.

I sit near him a little longer to see if he has anything to add. When he doesn't, I run off after Julian, smiling to myself in gratitude that I've released my truth, and it is now intertwining with our family.

25 | living on the moon

When June tenth finally arrives, I feel like I'm facing the last of the firing squad. This will be my first time declaring our desire to transfer this embryo with the BRCA1 gene to my IVF doc, and I'm nervous as to whether or not he will have an opinion. Because there is still a smidgen of me seeking encouragement—that what I'm doing is right, okay, safe.

But I'm more determined than ever! I tell myself while driving over. It is a sunny day in the Mission Bay area of San Francisco, and it smells like summer, tendrils of fog from SoMa just leaving the sky.

When I get to his office, my doc and I have an instant ease with each other. We ask after one another's families. He tells me a funny story about his kids asking what he does for a living and we share a laugh, our personal lives now overlapping.

"Gosh, you've been my doctor for nearly ten years now," I say.

"Your *favorite* doctor," he emphasizes.

"Ha!" *Maybe today he is.* I smile.

"Okay, well, you're back for transfer number three, I see."

"Yes, is that crazy?" *Why do I keep using that word?* I shake my head.

"It is! How can anyone handle three?" he jokes.

"Oh, you don't think it's crazy that I want to transfer the embryo with the BRCA gene?" I bravely spell out.

"No, what would be crazy is a three-for-three outcome."

"What?" He's lost me.

"Like, the odds," he says, shifting to the science, "of three for three successful transfers. I mean, we've had two for two," he shifts back, his tone jovial, "which is outstanding. But I'd be one hell of a doc to transfer a third and it be successful!"

My mind tries to catch up.

"Wait. Do you think we can do this? Be successful in a third transfer?"

"Oh, yes, yes, of course!" he scoffs. "I wouldn't be in this position if I didn't. Just know, I'm a really good doctor if we get three for three."

Hmm. I don't reply but try to pull a face that reflects agreement. I guess I really did come here expecting a different kind of validation—that transferring our BRCA1 embryo isn't cause for as much a pause as we originally thought—but he just skipped over it completely.

Should that be alarming to me? I can't quite determine if I should keep pushing for his opinion or not.

"So, when are we looking at here?" he asks into the silence.

I decide to stay the course of this conversation and ignore that my confidence just got chipped away a bit.

"Well, we'll be out of town at the end of this month into July—so, would August work?"

"Sounds good to me." He smiles. "I'll let my care team know."

He stands up to give me a hug.

I guess we're done here.

"That was weird," I tell Mark afterward.

"Well, do you still want to proceed?" he asks, not sure what he's navigating.

Am I wavering? Does he think I'm wavering? I won't let myself waver.

"Yes, I do," I state confidently, even though new questions are appearing in me. *Have I made too many assumptions? Have I not thought this through enough? Am I just having a wobble?*

I remember the positives I felt today and land there instead, where I'm still grounded and want to push forward.

"Perhaps that was just his way of being chummy with me?" I add.

"Perhaps," he concedes, and we keep the plan in play.

On the boys' last day of school, a neighbor reveals to me her and her husband's plan to move to Austin, Texas at the end of the year. Even though they are renovating their home up the road, they've run into so much red tape with the county that they are frustrated with the indeterminable costs and delays. Plus, with school fees and caring for her aging parents, their ample funds are only getting them so far in the Bay Area.

These echo some of our own thoughts that we haven't aired out loud. Some of the background noise that causes Mark and I to do our own family checks-ins where we re-up our goals and hone our vision of what is best for our boys, our lifestyle, and our future trajectory. So far, we keep landing on "All is going well, for now, let's stay," but with commutes getting longer, housing prices going up, and our motion toward a third transfer, we aren't entirely certain how long staying in the Bay Area will remain sustainable.

"Would you ever, say, move to Australia?" the neighbor ventures, while our kids are engaged in a game of red light, green light on our back deck.

"No way," I quickly admonish, half-looking at her. "That feels *so* far-fetched. Like living on the moon!" I add, because I haven't even had one sliver of an idea of living there. Ever.

"But," she pushes, "with your upcoming trip—I figured it was an option?"

Oh yes, our upcoming trip. I think of how Mark is often telling us how lovely Manly is—a beach town only a ferry ride from Sydney. How reminiscent of South Africa it is for him, and that he'd like to share it with us, since he's been there a few times over the last couple of years for work. We've managed to get tickets to tag along on his next trip, but this is really to give us something fun to do as a family of four in the long months of summer. A last hurrah before we become five.

"Nah," I tell her. "We're just making an excuse to join him and see what all the fuss is about," I say, knowing she often frequents Europe in the summer to do something similar.

"Ah," she says with a side-eye. "Do you think you're lifers here, then?"

"Well...I wish," I say, shrugging, keeping my eyes on the kids. The truth is, I don't know how solid our surroundings are, and I haven't yet told her about our plans for a third child.

That doesn't seem to satisfy her question, though, because she pushes with a "But, do you?" question, wanting to draw a parallel in me to what she is feeling, trying to decipher our connective tissue.

"It really is wonderful here. But if it *does* become unsustainable," I offer, "then we'd probably move to Colorado..." This is a side discussion Mark and I have had a few times prior, thinking of built-in support for a third child. "To be closer to family," I add.

The following week, we land at 9:00 a.m. in Sydney's T1 terminal. Stepping off a pleasant overnight flight on Qantas, it's a day and a half in the future. After we gather our bags and walk out into the damp, cool air—beside a courtyard full of native grasses, palms, and plants—I think, *How lucky are we to be here?*

We pack into a taxi that drives us to our Airbnb in Manly. We ride through a long tunnel under the Harbour Bridge, past quaint suburbs reminiscent of storefronts found in Wimbledon, and along hills that look out onto different waterways full of beautiful homes and greenery, much like Sausalito in Marin.

It's Australia's winter, and we've arrived after a rainstorm. When we pull into the driveway of our apartment for the next few weeks, we see it is half a block from the oceanfront. After hauling our stuff into the unit, the boys take off sprinting in their rainboots to splash in the puddles along the promenade next to the long stretch of sand.

It takes a few days for me to get oriented. I have to figure out how to entertain the boys when Mark's in the office, and the rain returns, drumming down. I also become more comfortable as a stand-out with my accent, for the first time feeling how Mark must feel with his South African one in the US. A friendly neighbor helps me turn a corner by dropping off some hand-me-down toys and books, along with the advice to "run 'em ragged, eat bananas, and get out in the sunshine"—when it appears.

And the sunshine does appear. Some beautiful rainbows, too. Around Manly, the boys climb on beachside boulders, dig with seashells, and walk fearlessly beside flocks of cockatoos clawing around the grass next to the sidewalks. We snack on banana bread with mascarpone cream, try warm Portuguese tarts, and become connoisseurs of avocado toast and babyccinos with chunky pink marshmallows on top. We get to know the rhythms of our street, like the daily feeding of nearly a hundred rainbow lorikeets at the house with the koi pond in front.

We venture farther out, too. We take ferry boat rides into Circular Quay to explore the city, the aquarium, and the zoo. We hop on a bus up to Newport to check out different sights past the beach towns of Dee Why, Collaroy, and Curl Curl. The boys find a fake podium where they pose for pictures at the top, labeled *legend* rather than *first* or *gold*.

We do well, our little team.

On our last day, walking back to our Airbnb alongside Cabbage Tree Bay, amid a clear sky and sparkling ocean, I feel inspired to say, "Wow, I could actually live here."

"See? See how nice it is?" Mark says.

"Yes, I really do," I say as the sun glitters off the water. "Thanks for sharing this place with us."

A couple of days later, seated on the wooden half-wall in front of our flower boxes, I'm policing the boys as they determine who gets to use the hose nozzle and on what setting. This is a typical afternoon occurrence for a warm day—this or whose turn it is on the popping toy mower or at the water table pump.

The sun is making its lazy summer descent across the hedges when Mark opens the screen door and walks over.

"Hey," he says, sitting next to me.

"What's up?" I ask, quickly telling the boys to keep the water on our side of the fence and out of the neighbor's garden.

"An opportunity came up that I want to run by you…" His knees knock into mine.

Julian has the hose and is spraying a wide stream into our grass, so I position myself toward Mark, giving him my full attention.

"I could work in Sydney for the next year."

"Whoa! Wait. Really?" I have to admit, my knee-jerk reaction is curiosity. "What does that look like exactly?"

"Well, they could use my presence in our office there…" An openness appears behind his gray-blue eyes that mirror the sky. "And we'd all move out together, for a year."

"Interesting…"

"But I'd only do it if you guys are with me. It'd be our adventure."

"Just a sec, while I digest this," I say, matching his excitement. It is not lost on me that I am facing the same question in the same place as with our neighbor a month ago, and now there is definite weight to it. But it feels less like pressure, more like mystery.

Kind of a delicious mystery.

"Here is the thing, though," he continues, taking an audible inhale. "I'd have to be there, up and running, by September first."

"Wowza." My breath catches. "That's a month away!" I bide a little time for my mind to catch up. "Okay, let's think on this. When do you have to let them know?"

"Mmm, the sooner the better."

"Well, how are you feeling about it?"

"I'm excited," he reveals, not often one to jump into anything, "as it is really a one-time thing."

"Huh, I wonder why that is."

"It's rare to get the opportunity to work in Australia at my age—and fits with the moment in the company's trajectory, I suppose." He shrugs.

"Well, weirdly, I kind of feel excited, too," I admit, coming off our visit and feeling drawn to trying something new among a less-populated, foreign lifestyle. "I think we should go for it."

"You do?"

"I do." Feels like an easy yes. *That's odd.*

"Let's sleep on it and decide tomorrow," Mark says, true to form.

Hmm. *Is there a double meaning in this? Am I escaping something here?* I stop to ask myself, Imogen. I really do. I receive a clear *no* in response.

What about the boys' school? Our embryo?!

The questions come at me hard and fast. These are the two things I hold like lifelines. But I find myself impenetrable.

Strange.

The school, our embryo—they aren't going anywhere, a voice reminds me. We can return to all these moving parts after a year.

This possibility feels like a breath of fresh air blowing into the year ahead. A breath where I can release my stronghold on being in control and relax.

Plus, stepping through this new door as a family feels really fun, and I could do with more fun.

Come September, we return to the same Airbnb we stayed at in July. It took a lot of effort to get here—untangling ourselves from all the commitments, all the *stuff*—but stepping onto Australian soil feels joyful, uncomplicated. The boys run up the familiar steps on the side of the building, pull the key from under the mat, and reclaim their same beds as last time. And once we hear the cockatoos screech on our balcony and see the sun cast shadows through the resident frangipani tree, we feel like we're home.

Interesting.

We quickly return to our previous states: me as that loud American, shouting after the boys to "Wait for me!" when they take off down the shoreline, feeling the sand in their toes and bringing it back into their beds later, and Mark starting most of his mornings in the ocean, swimming a satisfying 1.5 kilometers around the point to Shelly Beach and back. He is more effervescent and full of life than I've seen him in years—free of his hour-plus commute to Redwood City and looking forward to his twenty-minute ferry ride into the office in Sydney. We remark regularly on how the stressors of the Bay Area melt away in this solid dose of sunshine. We feel so far away from it all.

Yet, at night, when we can hear the waves crashing on the shore from our bedroom, I wonder, *Will we become friends, me and the sea?* Because a new sensation has also started to creep up, heightening the burgeoning reality that we are all we have here: an instinct to keep everyone close.

Perhaps that is why the shift from arriving to finding and entering school is a rocky one for me. The boys feel it, too. I haven't yet released my grasp on what I know and am familiar with to let them go into the open arms of this new experience.

I'd like to think of myself as adaptable, but also, as having the experience in life to find my way through unchartered waters with ease and grace.

Sadly, Imogen, this is not the case for me from the get-go as a parent in Australia.

There are a few recalibrations I have to make in regard to school and medical care here right away. Recalibrations that I'm unable to master from the first try. Or the second. Or even the third.

Before we arrived, I was quite pleased with myself. I'd found a school akin to the one the boys attended in Marin—a Montessori school that I was sure would warmly receive them. Attending a similar, internationally-accredited school as a child myself, I loved the synchronicity of it all: classrooms having familiar materials no matter what language was spoken, nor what decade of life we were in. The pedagogy stood. The schools who got it, I thought, were rare and coveted diamonds in the rough.

I had a pretty picture painted in my mind that we would step from the black-and-white hecticness of releasing our "things" in California, to a Technicolor world across the Pacific. One reaching out its hand to pull us into its vibrant spectrum. Like, *We know you. We are the same.*

Yeah, no.

First of all, the boys were in an age group at their old school called Primary, which encompassed the two-and-a-half to six-year-olds. In Primary, they transition to kindergarten in that final year of the mixed-age classroom. Here, I quickly gather, Primary is what they call their elementary school age group, for kindergarten through sixth grade. Preschool is anything prior.

Preschools also run on a part-time model, offering classes Monday through Wednesday or Thursday and Friday, rarely accommodating the five-day-a-week schedule that we'd grown accustomed to in the US. Even at this Montessori school I was so excited about.

The school year also begins at the end of January or early February and runs on a four-term schedule, each term being ten weeks with a two-week holiday between terms, except for the summer holiday, which is six to seven weeks long. Sigh.

When we arrive, it is midway through their third term. I haven't been guaranteed any spots for the boys but organize a tour at the school I found anyway, hoping I can win over the admissions director, or enrollment officer as she's called here, with my knowledge and personality. I hope she'll find, in meeting me, that their community would be getting an aligned family. And that the boys can start right away.

When Mark is able to be with the boys one afternoon, I find a bus that will drop me near the school. On a map, it is about twenty minutes away by car. The bus takes twice as long. I tell myself maybe it will feel faster on the way back.

Walking with the enrollment officer from room to room, she tells me she has a place for Julian in one of their Thursday-Friday groups. This gets my hopes up and I inwardly pat myself on the back for having shown up, only to find her add in the next breath, "but only starting in February."

I groan. Coming off two and a half months of summer break already, February feels like a long time to wait. But, the more I observe, the fonder I become of this place. Seeing their established classrooms and meeting with the head teacher, who has worked in the US and the UK, makes me feel like I've found a home away from home. I'm not ready to let go of the option.

We circle back to the enrollment officer's desk and I ask her, "What about Gideon? You haven't mentioned where he would be."

She sits at her computer to check her records. "What age did you say he was again?"

"He'll be five in February."

"Ah, so in his kindergarten year…"

Huh? I think. That doesn't make sense. "Already?"

"In Australia," she tells me, "if a child turns five before the thirty-first of July, he or she may begin their kindergarten year— and most do. However, it is the law that they are *in* primary school by age six."

"Okay," I say, even though I don't fully understand.

She types in a few things and keeps her eyes on her screen. "Ah, yes, like I thought. No, we don't have any spots available for Gideon."

I do not take this information at face value. *Surely there will be some wiggle room over the summer,* I think, having volunteered in the admissions department of our old school.

"Can't we just pay the application fee and get him on a waitlist?" I ask. I feel like I'm on the phone with the IVF office all over again—trying to wriggle my way onto their schedule earlier.

"No, you can't," she says. "Our kindergarten class is full, and we have a waitlist already that is a whole class full of students long."

No sugar-coating here.

I make this mental adjustment, tapping my teeth with my fingernail. She sits there across from me as I stare ahead, desperate for something promising to hold onto, unsure of how to manifest another option or bridge this gap that is widening between us.

"But," she offers, "the good news is that the public schools here are all great. Your son will get a whole buffet of friends to choose from. It's also a big expat community in Manly, and people love it. You'll be fine."

That is something, I think, but it isn't enough to curb my assumption that we'd get in anywhere we came across that matched our experience. Instead, I feel forced to come to terms with the idea of a larger public school for Gideon at age five, when he is only four—and I don't like it.

"Well, shall we sign up Julian then to secure his spot?" she asks, interrupting my thoughts. "I can't guarantee it will be available after today," she adds, trying to keep me engaged with what actually *is* available.

I want to commit but just can't right now. I'm still stuck in disappointment, unable to pivot. "Can you send me the paperwork, please? I have to get back," I say. I smile, trying to make a friendly exit, already anxious about how long it will take me to get back to relieve Mark. "Thanks so much for the tour. And for your candidness."

I truly am thankful for that, even though I am still unable to trust it.

When I return home, I look over the paperwork for Julian, seeing what I can do—other than pay the deposit—to hold onto our spot, while my mind plays catch-up. I see that the school needs proof of his vaccinations. I scan the signed copy I'm proud of myself for remembering to collect before we left and send that over.

I get a swift email back rejecting it.

What? I think. Again, this makes no sense. Usually I'm rewarded for being so on top of things. I quickly pick up the phone to ask her why it didn't work, wondering if the scan came up blank. I forgot to check.

"It isn't an AIR. That is what we need," she says.

"What is an AIR?"

"An Australian Immunisation Register, for proof of vaccines."

"Okay, well, clearly we're from the US and only have proof from our pediatrician there." I try to keep my tone neutral, even though I feel my frustration rising.

"Yeah, well, New South Wales won't recognize that."

"Okay, so how do I get what you need?" I let out a slow breath.

"With your Medicare number."

"I don't have a Medicare number," I say, thinking it should be obvious, feeling so out of my depth. Then I realize it might be helpful to add that we're not Australian citizens.

"Well, you still should be able to get an AIR. All children who attend school in Australia have to have one."

"Okay, well, then, how do you think I can get the actual sheet you need? Sorry, I just have no clue," I admit, still not following.

"You will have to go to a nurse at a GP's office to have them put your records in the system."

Finally, we're getting somewhere, I think.

I call the number of the family practice nearby that the enrollment officer recommended, feeling somewhat relieved until I find out that the nurse there doesn't have any availability for a few weeks. I'm also told I'll first need to join the practice in order to be seen.

"Okay, sign us up, then," I tell the receptionist. "We'll get our well checks done with you when we need them," I say, not wanting to waste the referral.

"Oh, well checks? We don't do those," she says. Turns out, no one in Australia does. Doctors here only see children if they're sick or have a specific condition to address.

Again, I'm learning. This is starting to feel like a wild goose chase.

"You can try one of the clinics in Manly to see a nurse there," she says. "The AIR records are accessible to all of the nurses and doctors in the state," she adds, then hangs up.

Later in the day, we find a medical center around the corner from our Airbnb that accepts walk-ins. The boys are thrilled to discover a box full of old toys in a small nook of the waiting room. They play with different cars on the carpet and on the walls while we wait.

When we're called back, the nurse looks at the sheets with the boys' vaccines and their dates, running them against her schedule. The dates, though, are implemented differently Down Under (to be fair, this is the same in any Commonwealth country). They start with the day first, then month, then year, so it takes a while for her to compare the boys' records with the New South Wales requirements.

The boys get antsy and have a hard time sitting still, having left the toys behind. They interrupt her with questions about the nearby machinery. This doesn't seem to bother the nurse, as she just ignores them, but it bothers me as I try to keep their hands off the equipment.

"Looks like they each need to have a vaccine," she eventually says. "Implementing all these dates is going to take me a while. I'll get them inserted and email the AIR to you next week."

"Not any sooner, by chance?" I ask.

"I am the only nurse here and work Tuesdays and Thursdays."

"Oh, okay. Thanks," I say, taking another deep breath as I note her immediacy is unmatched to what I've grown accustomed to in the US. Nevertheless, I am grateful we are making some progress.

"All right, let's start with Julian," she continues, looking back down at her sheet.

I coax Julian into my lap. He hops up and takes it all in—the nurse preparing the needle, asking him which arm is his dominant one—staring, mute, as I answer for him.

"Do you have one of those handy ShotBlocker tools?" I ask, recalling the way he is used to receiving shots back in Marin.

"Nooo, sorry, I don't know what that is," she says and injects him. The needle goes in more, well, obviously.

Julian screams.

"Do you want a lolly?" she asks, pointing to a container filled with unwrapped gummy snakes.

Ugh. How many fingers have been in that jar? I don't want to know...

He nods through tears and picks one. It helps, so I don't fight the germ battle today. Gideon follows shortly with his shot and happily selects a gummy snake as well.

When we walk back into our unit, I feel finished. Like an old dog learning new tricks. I just want to collapse on the sofa, close my eyes, and sink into oblivion.

The waves crashing in the background no longer register in my psyche and the enchantment of having a new experience in a new country quietly fades away.

To set ourselves up for success, we quickly get Australia-based phone numbers, a PO box, and open a bank account—with Commonwealth Bank. How mystifying that after that night years ago when I found the lump working on a banner ad for them, now I'm *their* client.

I also let go of the Montessori school altogether when I find a "long day care" for Julian—a preschool with a spot for him three days a week that serves a hot lunch (*score!*) and is walkable from our new apartment (we moved, because our favorite Airbnb was already booked out for the coming months).

Within a couple of weeks, I also find a spot for Gideon at a local preschool that feeds into the public school where he can begin kindergarten in the new year. Right when he turns five (*gulp!*).

Julian's long day care only begins next month, so Gideon is the first to do school in Australia. We take our double stroller to the bus, make our way down a small hill, and arrive on the earlier side. As I get Gideon situated into his classroom and he meets his teachers, one introduces him to another American boy—from Seattle—who is relatively new and a few other classmates who are there early as well. Gideon sits on the carpet beside them, grabs some magnetic blocks, and starts building. Julian and I say our goodbyes and head home.

At pick up, Gideon is in a cheerful, chatty mood. He tells me that he's made a new friend from the Netherlands. On our way out, I meet a Canadian mom whose daughter just started at the school, too.

Wow, this is quite an expat community, I think as the boys and I make our way over to a small swing set at the wharf. They climb into the side-by-side seats for me to push them, and we watch the different boats come and go as we wait for Mark to return on the fast ferry from the city. Soon Gideon hops off and twists the chains around Julian's seat so he can spin and spin.

I sit on a bench behind them, noticing the huge branches above our heads and the wide girth of the Moreton Bay fig tree they extend from. The lorikeets chirp around us and I sigh, feeling like we've made it to the end of our first normal-seeming day in this still very new-to-us part of the world.

Mark joins us for Gideon's school drop-off the next morning. We're a family of four marching down Manly's central shopping area, the Corso, full of good feelings on the heels of yesterday's wins. No shops are open yet, and there are only a few individuals dressed for the workday, heading to the ferry. A surfer with his board walks by in a wetsuit; another pedals by with his board attached to the side of his bike.

As we get closer to the bus stop across the street, Gideon leaps out of his bottom seat in the double stroller and runs in the opposite direction—back toward the beach. He is at least ten paces away by the time Mark and I look at each other and he takes off after Gideon, while I stay with Julian.

The background noise—a lone kookaburra cackling like a

monkey that no one thought twice about—now becomes Gideon screaming that he is "NOT going back to school!"

My heart races at the terror of him pounding his fists on Mark's back, increasing his volume to *let him go*, but I try not to panic or draw any further attention to the drama unfolding.

Back at the stroller, Mark and I buckle him in with a two-on-one approach. I calmly tell him, "You *are* going to school today, Gideon. There are only two more days to go. It is a short week, I know it is new…"

He fights me, squirming to get out, not soothed at all.

"And Daddy is really excited to come see where you are and have you show him your new classroom," I finish.

More kicking, screaming, and inconsolable emotions erupt.

Maybe I shouldn't have mentioned him showing Mark around? I second-guess myself, scrambling to find the best way to get him through this and to school on time, when he breaks free from the stroller straps again and takes off running. Harder and faster this time. Mark turns around to catch him, and I follow, jogging behind with Julian buckled into the other seat in the stroller.

The physicality of the moment quickly comes to a crescendo that feels insurmountable. I imagine us chasing him all the way to the water and him jumping in to escape the day's realities. *We just need to get him to the bus*, I tell myself to keep my composure, when I notice Mark has a hold of him again. I catch up to them.

"Gideon," I say as calmly as I can, "you may sit in the stroller or Daddy can keep carrying you—what would you like?"

But he is flooded and unable to answer.

"Okay, we will help you get there," I announce as Mark keeps him steady along his chest. He holds him there until they are on the bus and seated. I clunkily get the stroller folded up and tucked in behind them, while holding Julian. The quiet, contained public space snaps Gideon out of his rebellion and he resigns himself to silence for the ride.

When we get off at our stop, Gideon holds my hand and walks beside me. It feels like a miracle when we make it through the school doors in a civilized manner. We are nearly late, and the classroom is full of students.

Mark walks around, checking out the shelves and set-out activities with enthusiasm that Gideon watches in stillness and silence. When it is time for us to say goodbye, tears drain out of him, along with dramatics, again.

His teacher—who is Danish, tenured, and calm—assures us this is very normal for the second day and that he will be okay. She encourages us to go. Her eyes are caring and compassionate. We step away and say goodbye but, once outside, feel torn to shreds.

"Dang, that was difficult," I say.

"Like the last chopper out of Saigon!" Mark says, exasperated.

While hoofing it up the hill to catch the bus back into Manly, I say, "I can't even imagine being pregnant or having a baby with us right now." Sweaty from the warming spring weather, I add, "And what if the embryo splits and we have twins?"

My mind spins as these thoughts hang over me, along with the physical and emotional exhaustion of the morning.

"Yeah, but we don't have to think about those things now, Lindsay," Mark says. "These challenges are all part of the deal. Remember Mila saying it took her two years to adapt to California when she first moved there? It took me a while, too."

"True," I say, catching a view of the ocean butting up against the endless horizon. *We're not even going to be here after a year*, I tell myself, like a mantra.

By December, we've moved again to another new apartment. The previous one proved to be too small, too proximate to others without children, and, frankly, too stressful for me and the boys to be confined in while Mark was away at work or in California for a board meeting. When a larger, more private and inviting space appeared, I jumped on it. Leaped, actually.

It is in this new, third space that the boys and I experience our first warm Christmas. We join the family from Seattle for a picnic on the beach among Aussies in Christmas-sweater-printed swim shirts and shorts with koalas wearing Santa hats. We also make it through a season of horrendous fires. And, come January, there is a debate building in the background about a virus spreading from China called COVID-19 and whether or not it will reach us.

Mid-February 2020, Gideon transitions to kindergarten with ease, and Julian's new year at his long day care is off to a good start. I deliberately pass on becoming a room parent for either of their classrooms, knowing by mid-June we'll be flying back to or through San Francisco.

Speaking of which, I start wondering, *Uh, where, exactly, will we go?*

We no longer have a house waiting for us in California. We've spoken of visiting my family in Colorado to collect some, if not all, of the boxes of things that they're holding for us, but we aren't necessarily wanting to live there, yet.

Nevertheless, I am eager for a plan. You're in the back of my mind, Imogen, still hovering there, and I'm ready to bring you to the forefront. It is hard for me to get anything definitive out of Mark, who is very immersed in the now, where his Sydney-based job is still very demanding and time-consuming. But I angle for *something* from him to hold onto when an idea appears.

"What if we schedule our transfer for when we're in Colorado this year?" I ask him, already assuming we'll book tickets to spend a few weeks there, at least.

"Why do you say that?"

"Well, for one thing, we have a place to stay with my parents and help with the boys during appointments. Plus, it'll be summer, so my sister and her kids will be around, too. I'm sure my dad will know someone he could point us toward," I add, ready to keep generating reasons.

"You could look into it," Mark says, then hesitates. "But the bigger question is—can we handle it?"

Why is he airing the dirty laundry of this huge adjustment we just went through? I think, clenching my teeth. Yes, our boys have exhibited a whole gamut of behaviors in adjusting to our almost-year here, but that's because there's been so much change without any real anchor.

"I just feel like we're running out of time," I confess as my heart sinks at the thought of missing out on you entirely, Imogen, "and if we schedule it for then—in a place I know we'll be—I feel like it will actually happen."

"I get that."

"And if we don't, something else will fill the space and I'll lose my grasp on her…"

I feel tears forming and take a deep breath, not wanting the emotion to leak into my plea.

"Okay, see what you can find out," he says.

Great, I will! I think, instantly flipping a switch.

I leave Mark at his computer and step into another room to call my dad, now retired. He refers me to a doc he knows and likes in Denver who also happens to be working with his previous longtime embryologist.

I spend the next few weeks emailing him and his office to see if we can organize a transfer for June. I ask his nurse, and double-check with my dad, if it is risky to fly our embryo over from San Francisco. Both assure me they ship and receive embryos all the time and that part of the process is very low risk.

The more I look into it, the easier it seems to make it happen.

A few days later, I sit on the edge of our bed just feet away from Mark at his desk, overlooking the palm tree-lined street as I share all the encouraging details with him.

"Okay, let's proceed," he agrees.

I step away feeling my entire insides expand, satisfied with this destination to look forward to. I now have the energy I need to get us through these last four months and into June. I sign some paperwork that releases my files and our embryo from my doc in SF. I shoot off an email to my old doc's care team to keep them informed.

I sleep soundly, knowing these next steps are in place.

In March, there is more talk of COVID-19 spreading to more countries. A conference Mark had planned to attend at the end of the month gets postponed. We sigh in relief that he won't get stuck there, then decide he wouldn't have gone anyway.

One quiet weekday, we go into the CBD (central business district of Sydney) for a medical examination for Permanent Residency (PR) visas that Mark's company has sponsored. We figured doing so was a fortunate sort of insurance policy for us to partake in. Unfortunately, having sat by a guy with a hacking cough on the ferry ride there, Mark and the boys catch a cold.

A couple of days later, their throats burn, and they have high fevers and the worst migraine-like headaches they've ever had in their lives. When Julian can't kick his symptoms, we ask a doctor for a COVID-19 test, but seeing as we haven't traveled overseas recently ourselves, he won't give us one—nor would he prescribe anything differently if he did.

"Just take Panadol and rest," we're told (Panadol is the Tylenol equivalent in AUS).

We keep tabs on the news each night before bed and each morning when we wake.

By April, Australia is in full lockdown.

It begins over the boys' fall school holidays. Residents are only allowed to leave their homes for essential reasons (health care and the like), outdoor gatherings are limited to two people, and outdoor exercise is confined to one hour per day within two kilometers of your home. We take turns pairing up with the boys to go on outside excursions around the neighborhood. We spot bush turkeys on telephone wires and strung-up, unused kayaks bobbing in a row on the bay.

Our flight to SF gets canceled.

Maybe we'll just push the transfer back, I think as the weeks pass and we learn, too, that the boys won't be returning to school in mid-April after their break.

The air becomes universally palpable with stress as we don't know what changes are coming, nor what—at all—to anticipate.

Mark's office closes and our walls fill with tension as he logs on to Zoom calls and tries to drown out the noise from the boys that carries down the tall interior corridor of our old building. Police horses walk through the streets. Helicopters patrol the area at night, shining spotlights on the pavement below, to confirm people aren't out breaking the stay-at-home orders. Our only consolation is that a version of this is happening back home. Plus, we've been awarded PR, so are thankful to find some comfort in the fact that we won't be kicked out of the country anytime soon. Not that it has come to that, but you never know.

By the end of June, it feels too risky to uproot and try to rebook a flight to the US, only to stay indoors there and be among a higher number of cases. Around the time we have this thought, the airlines start to offer deferring flights for six months to a year. We decide to do just that and remain in Australia until December—the end of the school year. We'll reassess then and see how everything is going.

Then, all flights get grounded coming in and out of Australia anyway.

I email the Colorado doc to pause our upcoming transfer.

Our embryo stays in SF.

By mid-July, classrooms are back in session and there is a collective sigh of relief. We have some restrictions, but kids aren't required to wear masks at school, and social distancing is loosely enforced. We are all so desperate to interact that small groups of us linger longer at the local playgrounds to compare notes and share our euphoria in the fact that our children get to play together again.

One overcast day, I'm in the kitchen putting away dishes and see the number for Gideon's school pop up on my phone.

Uh oh, this can't be good, I think as my heart rate spikes and I set some glasses down to press *answer.*

"This is Lindsay."

"Hi, Lindsay. Gideon had a fall," the school secretary tells me, calmly and kindly. "We didn't see what happened, but he says he tripped and landed on a stick. The skin on his chin is cut open and bleeding. Please come quickly—he may need stitches."

"Is he okay? How is he doing?" I ask, my heart in my throat.

"He is being very brave and isn't crying anymore but has had quite a shock."

I arrive within minutes to find my five-year-old sitting in a small space next to the front office on a light blue sick bed, sleepy and out of it. He has a big bandage plastered to his chin and is being tended to with compassion. Just so sweet, my little boy.

His eyes, dilated and drained, meet mine.

"Hey, monkey," I say, trying to spark some life back into him across the room of foreign accents. "Let me help you get to the car and we'll go to the doctor together." I lean down to pick up his backpack and set my hand on his back to slow my own battering heartbeat.

I'm not sure how to best get to the other side of all this but say, "Mommy's got this" to inspire confidence in us both.

"His shirt is in here," the secretary tells me, handing me a bulky plastic shopping bag tied with a knot. "I'm not sure if it is salvageable, but we gave him a clean one from our secondhand shop. You can keep it."

For all the times I've been in to fill out paperwork, I haven't seen this more tender side of her before. I stop to appreciate her kindness.

"Thank you," I say and help Gideon up into a side hug.

He and I stay smooshed together as we walk the block to the car.

After getting through triage, we are directed to a bed in a long empty row of beds in the emergency pediatric ward of the hospital. Gideon and I take a seat and sit in silence.

Will I get to watch a show? he asks me. I tell him I don't know.

A nurse and a very young-seeming doctor come over to clean his wound. When the doctor removes the bandage, the skin is uneven and flappy. I watch her inquisitive assessment and see the timidness in her own eyes amplify behind her oversized trendy glasses.

I inhale to steady my own pulse and keep from diving in to protect Gideon. But what would I say, really? I just don't trust her. I hold Gideon's hand as she pulls more of the bandage away from his wound and touches his skin.

"It's going to need stitches," the doctor says loudly.

Uh oh, this one hasn't had much experience with kids, I think and respond with a quiet, "Okay, thanks"—an unspoken request for her to match my tone.

"I'm going to put some numbing cream on and then we'll get him into a room with some nitrous oxide—you know, laughing gas?—to help him with the procedure. You can come," she tells me, equally as loud as before.

I shake my head slightly when she walks away.

An hour later, the doctor leads us into a procedure room down the hall. Another young doctor, but with an air of more experience, plus an older nurse, join us. They don't waste any time getting a mask around Gideon's face so he can breathe in the laughing gas. He squirms and tries to get out of it.

"This is to help you relax," I tell him calmly, still holding his hand and trying to keep my panic at bay.

"So that you're not bothered by what we're doing," the new doctor says as he restrains my son and holds the mask over his face. I wince and hope Gideon doesn't notice.

The young female doctor gets a curved needle ready with the nurse's help and pauses, holding it in front of Gideon's chin.

"What do you think I should do?" she asks the male doctor as she moves in closer to study the jagged line. I squeeze my eyes shut briefly. *This fucking lady.*

"Go for the muscle, the sublayer, first."

She does, slowly. She is on to her second stitch when Gideon groans and wriggles some more. I stare.

"Mom looks like she is going to pass out," the nurse calls out. She turns to me. "Sit, put your head between your legs and breathe."

I lower myself to the floor, bend my neck and take in a few deep gulps of air, propping my elbows on my knees. I peek up to make sure Gideon is okay when I hear the male doctor say, "Oh no, that is not right—you didn't get it."

Oh my god, really?!

"You need to take those out and start over," he tells the doctor with the needle.

I dip my head down for one more deep breath, then rise to regrasp Gideon's hand at the side of the bed. The male doctor is forcefully holding the gas mask in place as Gideon fights it. I don't blame him. This is taking so long already.

"Hurry up, he can't be under the laughing gas much longer," the nurse warns the female doctor.

They are all trying to hold it together, but this is a shit show.

The female doc pulls out the old stitches. *My god, I might actually faint this time.* When she starts the new stitch, Gideon throws up.

It goes into his chin.

Fuck! I start to crumble inside, equating their incompetence to everything Australia: how I can't figure out the basic things in this country, how they don't feel as on top of things as I'd like them to be—as I expect myself to be in life by this age—and how I feel stuck here and not able to be in the US where I feel certain, down to my cells, that this sort of botched attempt wouldn't happen.

But I will myself to stay upright. Still thinking, on some level, that I am leading by example, not only for Gideon, but everyone in this room.

"Oh, no. Oh, no," the male doctor says.

"Just clean it out," the nurse tells him. When he doesn't move, she gets some saline, flushes out the vomit, and wipes at Gideon's shirt while the female doctor continues and the male doctor just gawks, holding the mask in place.

"Almost done, nearly there, it will be over soon…" I say soothingly to Gideon as I help hold him steady.

"We'll need to get him on a course of antibiotics," the male doctor turns to tell me. "In case there is any infection here."

Ya think? I just nod in agreement.

Finally, they finish.

"We'll keep him for a couple of hours just to make sure he doesn't get sick again," another nurse tells me when we return to the quiet corridor of hospital beds. Gideon lies down, and she finally turns on the television suspended above us. "We'd like him stable before he goes home."

Brushing my hand over his head, softening his hair, I lower myself onto the narrow mattress next to Gideon. He is in and out of sleep. He has gauze over his stitches and a bandage over that to keep the site clean and dry for the next week.

After an hour, a new nurse comes by with apple juice and a couple packets of saltine crackers. Gideon rips into them, hungry. When they don't come back up, he asks for more, and we are discharged.

That night, I sit in the dark on a step at the back end of our house, behind our kitchen.

There is a concrete storage room here and, a few months from now, I'll have a run-in with a hand-sized Huntsman spider that will jump out at me from a box and I'll scream and clamber up onto the nearby kitchen countertop. Mark will run in to help me, feeling like he saved the day—and my nerves.

But not tonight.

Tonight, I just cry. From exhaustion, from the shock, from not being able to help Gideon today other than being a witness.

Nobody hears me, nor do I want anyone to hear me.

In this quiet moment to myself, my brave face slips off, and it dawns on me that a lot of the doing—when it comes to the kids—falls on my shoulders, into my hands. Mark does what he can when he can, but it's really up to me to make the in-the-moment decisions and see them through.

Which makes me wonder, *Am I fooling myself here? Can I really handle another child? What else is around the corner?*

"I'd like to talk to an IVF specialist," I say to a general practitioner the following week after disclosing that we have an embryo in the US and are unable to get back for our planned transfer.

Time still feels crucial. I know I don't have the luxury of dragging my feet, and I need help to understand what is possible here—*if* anything is possible here—and whether or not I can handle it.

The GP hands me a couple of names, and after a quick Google search, I schedule a consult with the one that has the most positive reviews and is located closest to me. Doctors aren't fully back to seeing patients in person yet, and since an exam isn't required, we meet over Zoom.

When we log in, I see she, too, is in the comfort of her own home. It feels strangely intimate, accessing her personal life as I share mine—my history and questions. At one point, we're interrupted by her doorbell and she excuses herself to receive a package. I am wondering how present she really is when she sits back down in front of the screen and says, "An embryo can certainly be shipped internationally; we do it all the time."

I find this wild. Turns out this has been done internationally for over twenty years.

"There are a few cryo-shippers we use," she says. "One in particular, even, has worked with your clinic in San Francisco multiple times."

That is amazing, I think and notice her eyes divert to a space on her screen away from the camera. She tells me the shipper's name, and I write it down.

"Is this still being done with the travel restrictions right now?" I ask.

"Yes. This is under 'approved essential travel' and our lab is still receiving deliveries. Our shipper should be able to give you the latest information, though."

When our call ends, I immediately dial the international cryo-shipment company who has worked with the doctor's lab here and our doctor's lab in SF. A male coordinator answers. His voice gives me pause and I feel my guard going up, considering how much information I should give him, but he assures me they have, in fact, done this many times before. No question is too personal or one he hasn't heard before.

I become at ease enough to release the details that feel most precious to me: our one healthy embryo, a female that has BRCA1, who we'd like to bring all the way from San Francisco to Sydney.

That's you, kid.

I choke up. Again, here I am putting the possibility of your existence into the hands of others. Of this man. Of whatever airline flies you over. Of whatever human sits near your package to ensure your safety. It feels nuts but also like our only option. And an almost fantastical one at that, like a swirl of magic we are setting in motion, tended by many.

It takes a few more emails and calls—feeling somewhat embarrassed every time I have to explain myself to the next stranger—to receive a quote. The price is hefty enough for Mark and I to stop and reflect. It's basically an overseas plane ticket with extra care and hand-holding built in. Not quite business class, but close.

"What do you think?" I ask Mark.

"What do *you* think?" he asks back.

After feeling like I just stripped naked in front of all those people, hearing the numbers and letting the reality sink in, it is hard to step into a decision. Instead, I ask the coordinator for current lead times and when he'd need us to put down a deposit.

"Well, we are currently experiencing extensive delays in our orders and are at least two months out," he warns. "So, at this time, we can get you on a waitlist—without a deposit—and I'll call you when a flight becomes available."

This feels like just the answer I need to relax—and give myself the space for a clear yes or no to appear.

To be honest, I'm relieved you aren't coming on the next flight over, Imogen. I'm still trying to wrap my mind around what would come next and if I can even handle it: being pregnant here, getting the boys to school and myself to doctor appointments while Mark is working so heavily, having the hands to do it all back in the baby cave…

But I want to see where this leads.

We agree to get on the waitlist, and I email our lab in SF with the plan.

We're all on standby.

In September, the first Airbnb we stayed at goes up for rent and off Airbnb. I take a picture of the "For Lease" sign when I walk by and send it off to Mark, as we often think of the space fondly. With international flights still grounded, we've discussed not returning to the US—yet—and give ourselves permission to break our lease in favor of returning to our most-loved home in Australia thus far. It is warmer than our current place, closer to the beach, and has a peek-a-boo view of the ocean.

Within a month, we move back in—appreciating the space as a return to some welcome familiarity—and are instantly welcomed into a nook of friendly neighbors. The spot to our left even has two young kids our boys' ages. Soon they are joining us after school to throw paper airplanes or create chalk drawings together on our driveway out front.

One Friday, Mark finishes work early and hops onto our new secondhand boxy, red cargo bike to pick up Julian from school. The bike—where we can all feel the breeze on our faces and take turns making the *tring-tring* sound of the bell as we go—makes for a quicker, happier, commute than the double stroller. I stay back with Gideon, who is scootering in our driveway.

When they return, Julian jumps out to join Gideon on his own scooter, both of them doing laps out front, and I step over to Mark as he locks the bike back up in the garage. "How'd it go?"

"It was a bit concerning," he says, futzing with the bike key.

"What do you mean?"

"Well." He sighs, finally getting the key to cooperate. "When I got there, they didn't know where Julian was."

"What?" I say, wide-eyed. "Where was he?!"

"They said he'd just been at circle time and thought he was in the bathroom, but when they went to tell him I'd arrived, he wasn't there."

"Well, how did you find him, then?" I ask, my annoyance elevating. *Why isn't Mark as bothered as I am?*

"They said they were short-staffed and couldn't leave the group outside, so I just went in to look. I found him crouched behind a bookshelf in an empty classroom, with the lights off."

"Goodness! Was he okay?"

"Yeah, he told me he was hiding quietly so he couldn't be found," Mark delivers, unfazed.

"Weird. Do you think he didn't want to be there?" This conversation is making me more and more unsettled.

"No, I don't think it was anything like that."

"Hmm. Was anyone concerned?"

"No. They were very chill about it."

"Who is *they*?" I name names, trying to jog his memory. Once I sort out who was in charge, I make a mental note.

We look over at Julian playing happily. He seems okay, but I quickly realize I am not okay. The teacher that we've loved and trusted most since Julian started recently moved schools for a better opportunity post-COVID, and I'm not liking what is left in her wake.

I'm telling you, Imogen, this would never fly in the US.

After the weekend, I ask the school's director about the incident, giving her the benefit of the doubt to apologize or console me. *Maybe they're still getting organized*, my mind offers as she considers my question.

"I didn't hear about that," she says instead. "No big deal, I guess."

What? A child is missing and no one noted or reported that the kid's dad found him hiding in the classroom?!

She offers nothing more, so neither do I. Why make a fuss if the person in charge isn't fussed? What difference will it make? As I walk away, uncomfortably leaving Julian in her care, I ask myself why I can't chill out.

Am I being too much of an American here? But he is only three—three!

That evening, while the boys are out front again, this time blowing bubbles, one of our neighbors on the other side of our building walks by with her two daughters.

They are drawn in, and I immediately take note of the mom's warmth and calm engagement with her children and my own. She tells me that she lived in the US for many years before returning home to Australia, where she is now teaching.

"Oh, you're a teacher," I say and share with her my discomfort over Julian's disappearance last week. "Do you think my reaction is ridiculous?"

"Not at all," she says, exasperated, and I feel my shoulders fall from my neck. "We would *not* have handled things that way, nor would it have been okay not knowing where he was in the first place."

I thank her.

After a few more exchanges—she with my boys, and me with

her girls—I ask, "Where is it that you work?"

"At a Montessori long day care over in Mosman."

"Wait, what?" I ask, quickly explaining my knowledge of Montessori and how hard I found it to get into the one nearby last year. I hadn't even thought to look in Mosman, being at least a twenty-minute drive—over a bridge. "How have you found the commute?"

"Really not bad. The school starts early enough and has flexible hours for families to avoid the busy driving times."

"Maybe I should look into it," I think out loud.

"We've actually had some spots open up after COVID. I'll send you my boss's email. Reach out and come take a look."

Wow, that was a lucky conversation, I think as we go our separate ways to get dinner started. *Maybe this place could offer us a more like-minded community.*

Within a week, we have Julian enrolled in a Thursday-Friday class at the Montessori school in Mosman. He has some initial resistance at drop-off, but finding our neighbor there relaxes him. I soon observe his confidence in choosing materials off the shelves and independence in working with them—everything from pouring to counting to sorting to cleaning.

It isn't long before the lead teacher pulls me aside and praises, "What a Montessori kid he is!"

This fills my heart as I drive away, knowing he is in an environment I understand and trust, and seeing him celebrated there, too. I feel like I made a good pivot.

The good feelings last as the weather warms up, and we plan on hosting a few friends for Thanksgiving. Mark makes the meal more South African than American by roasting a leg of lamb for the main dish, and the day of, he works from home so he can tend to his four-hour roast in our small oven.

Our friend Gelma ("Jell-muh"), who we know from our frequent visits to the coffee shop around the corner, is staying the night on the extra twin bed in Gideon's room, after dinner out with her friends and before flying home to Brazil the next morning. We all adore her and are happy to get in a little extra time together before she leaves.

Extending ourselves in these ways to new friends lately has made us feel more like our old selves.

"Bye, guys!" I say as Mark logs on to a Zoom call in our bedroom and Gideon tries to follow me out of the house, even though he has chosen to stay home while I drive to Mosman to get Julian.

"Where is Gelma?" Gideon asks, wanting to play a game with her before she leaves for dinner.

"I think she is in the garage packing her suitcase, monkey, but stay up here since Daddy is on a call and can't see you down there, okay?"

I leave him standing in the doorway, then head to the car and drive off.

I'm maybe a minute down the road when a call comes through from Mark.

"Did I forget something?" I laugh, answering on Bluetooth.

"He's doing okay now, but Gideon's finger got smashed in the front door and there was a lot of blood."

"Oh my gosh," I say as my heart sinks and my insides cringe. Our front door is heavy and fire-safe with a weighted, automatically slamming hinge. "Should I come back?"

"Well, I think he needs to see a doctor. I canceled my call. I can take him. The bleeding is under control now and he's calmed down. You go get Jules. But where do you think I should go?"

"Try to make it to the GP at the hospital because, if he needs an X-ray, it can happen across the hall there."

"Good call. I'll get an Uber to take us."

"What happened to Gelma?" I ask, thinking of her in the garage, hearing the screaming, possibly scared to come back inside.

"I don't know. She wasn't around. Must've already headed out."

Okay, phew. "Sounds like we need to call off Thanksgiving?"

"Yes. That reminds me, I've gotta turn off the oven."

"I'll text everyone when I get to Mosman. How about Julian and I meet you at the hospital?"

"Sounds good."

This hospital experience is a lot easier for Gideon and me both, but the injury still feels traumatic. Mark takes Julian home, and Gideon and I follow around 10:00 p.m., once the doctor declares Gideon will need a nail bed repair surgery the following morning.

He and I miss our in-person goodbye with Gelma, but the surgery goes well, and Gideon receives a boxer-looking mitt of a bandage wrapped around his whole right hand up to his elbow, and a sling to keep his finger elevated.

That evening, I feel like a flat tire. All the air propping me up has leaked out.

"I think our family is at capacity right now," I tell Mark once the boys are asleep. "Too many moving parts, too many surprises, not enough of you and me..."

Having experienced the injury firsthand and dealing with the on-the-spot juggle of coordinating everyone's immediate needs—all while having to neglect work, his nearly perfectly cooked meat, and a get-together that we all longed for—Mark gets it.

The pragmatic part of my brain is taking the lead. My emotions are asleep in the other room, and I'll go join them shortly for a much-craved early bedtime, but for now, all I can register is that our cart of what we can optimally handle in life is full. Maybe maxed out.

There is only one more potential surprise I know is coming.

Mark wraps me in a hug and kisses the top of my head.

"I'd like to get off the waitlist for cryo-shipping." I say, pulling back to tell him. "Just to release the pressure. So I don't have to unexpectedly be faced with the decision tomorrow, or next week. What do you think?"

"Makes sense."

"Yeah," I say with a sigh, squeezing his hand. "Let's see what the new year brings."

I still want you, dear Imogen, but it's like I need more limbs, more headspace, more understanding of my surroundings that I can't attain overnight. I haven't even yet gotten onto a preventative-measure train here for BRCA1, and in the back of my mind, I know I'm due for my annual blood test and pelvic exam—not to mention dentist appointments for the boys and taking my own measurements of their height and weight to track their growth. Things that we'd already be doing if we were back in the US.

I am looking to next year for oxygen. It is only a few months away.

31 | who-knows-where

Oxygen comes in the form of community. When another COVID outbreak near the end of 2020 sends our local area into a second lockdown, our growing social circle is desperate to maintain connection. We deliver treats to one another to share from afar, orchestrate walk-by times to wave and catch up over our separate balconies, and fly paper airplanes with secret messages over the fence to the kids next door. We spend Christmas and New Year's Day on the beach with another family—groups of up to ten being allowed to gather outdoors. The boys boogie board and run around endlessly in the shallows, building piles of seaweed, entirely taking for granted that they have the shore to themselves.

When the lockdown ends two weeks later, I think, *That was actually a pleasant interlude!* and feel rather refreshed and unscathed by it all.

Once both boys are back in school—Monday through Friday now, for both of them—I find myself with more time than I've had in a while and more open to something new.

I try out a book club in Cremorne. We all read an Australian historical memoir, and I'm excited to discuss it—to hear and learn what others think. But I'm the youngest in the room by decades and unable to find a voice in common with the other attendees. I walk away feeling like a tolerated outsider.

Nah, I don't want to spend my energy this way, I think, driving home.

Instead, I look into helping out at the local library, to connect with others over my love of books there, but quickly learn that I need to attend another school and get another degree to even volunteer. *Australia just has so many different ways of doing things*, I think, a bit bummed this is too long a road for me to travel down.

I also contemplate doing an unpaid hour each week as an ethics teacher for Gideon's school, sharing with the director in my interview that I have hours to spare—which is what, a friend tipped me off, they need most. When the director brushes that offering off with "You're new here, that won't always be the case," I stop myself from pursuing the endeavor further.

That's right, Lindsay, I tell myself, again walking away. *Maybe that opening in you for your daughter is just around the corner.*

I plan our first exploratory trip—away from Sydney, to the Blue Mountains—for the winter school holidays. I look forward to the two-hour drive, cozy fireplaces, and maybe even a little snow come June and July.

In the meantime, we all (minus Mark, who is already at home in the water) get more comfortable in the ocean—the boys with their swimming skills and confidence, jumping over and ducking under waves both big and small, and me, in my bravery to venture farther out and do an open-ocean swim. The water is choppy, the current an energy to contend with, and even though I am unable to see the creatures beneath me—which causes me mild panic— I make it safely from shore to shore with the help of some patient and encouraging friends.

Despite the many starts and stops prior, this season brings a lot of happiness and promise for us, and as our experiences get lighter and more laughter-infused, my brain and body relax.

Then, one day, Gideon asks, "Mom, when is my sister coming?"

I'm caught off guard that he remembered. "Mmmm. Good question. I don't have an answer for you at the moment."

He returns to whatever he is doing, okay with not knowing. But this question retriggers my internal desire for you, Imogen, and I am unable to get back to whatever I was just doing.

I start talking about you waiting in the wings.

"What does Mark think?" a friend in California asks me over the phone.

"He seems on board if it is what I want."

"Okay, that is good. Definitely harder if you're not on the same page."

But is it? I'm left wondering when we hang up. *If he dug his heels into a no, would it make me want to fight for you more? Or, if he just had an easy yes, would I leap back to my own yes more effortlessly?*

And then, *Am I looking for permission to let you go? For someone else to make the decision for me?*

I am left standing back in the discomfort of indecisiveness.

"Having kids in Australia is so wonderful," a local expat friend insists over coffee one morning. "You must do it, no question. You get to sit on the beach. The babies love it."

"Yes, but her having the gene feels so heavy," I say. "It is what makes it hard for me to say yes so easily."

She just listens, because she doesn't know. But I appreciate hearing her easy yes so that I can try it on for size. It doesn't quite fit yet.

"And didn't you just get to walk home from the hospital?" I ask, remembering there used to be one up the hill that has since closed. "That was definitely an added convenience!"

"True," she says, "but the new hospital is so nice. What does it matter, really, that it is a twenty-minute drive away?"

Why does it feel so much farther than that, I ask myself, *and instantly isolating when I think about it?* Then I remember: We don't have family here, or backup, and my only experience of the hospital so far has been for emergencies.

I'm also worried that if something happens to me, Mark won't be able to get there, and I'll be on my own. Again with the emergencies. And now I'm right back to my old thoughts that a third child would mean a lot of solo parenting for me. *Dang, why do I feel like I keep hitting my head against a wall?*

It's like I want reality to be different, but it keeps showing me my limitations. I berate my internal compass, wanting to force its course.

"Maybe you should check in with someone again about your body?" Mark prompts when I'm home later, talking myself in circles. "We keep forgetting your pregnancies were hard on you, and now that more time has passed and we're in a new country, I wonder if it is a good idea. I worry about you, too."

It takes a few weeks, but after receiving a clear pelvic exam and no CA-125 markers in my bloodwork, I am referred to a gynecological oncologist. Being thirty-seven now, forty feels right around the corner, so I'm eager for the current guidelines regarding ovarian cancer prevention for BRCA1 carriers, as well as what his thoughts may be on a third pregnancy for me.

I drive an hour west to a who-knows-where suburb, truly feeling in foreign territory. But my determination for a recommendation gets me through a long, dark underground tunnel, past a few confusing intersections, and around a construction detour—to the oncologist's office.

The doctor is round-faced with a ready smile and greets me

with enthusiasm.

Strange, I think, feeling more skeptical than at ease in his presence.

Once I have a seat and he tells me he's read my file, I lead with, "When do *you* believe I should have my ovaries removed for ovarian cancer prevention? Because I'm thinking of transferring this BRCA1 female embryo I have and being pregnant for a third time."

"Oh, I think that is just wonderful! An embryo just like you!" He celebrates this news so quickly and with such warmth, I wonder if he is all there.

He isn't put off by BRCA1? I think. *Not bracing me for what could come because of my age and history?* And also: *Maybe I have more of a clue than the doctors here do.*

Again, my expectations and present reality seem to be oceans away.

"I see you've had a bilateral salpingectomy?" he continues.

"Yes, I've had my tubes removed."

"And you've taken birth control for the maximum preventative time at some point?"

"Yes, before my first pregnancy."

"And your cancer was hormone-receptor negative...so, really, you've done all we know for sure is the best protocol for prevention of ovarian cancer."

These questions are annoying to me and feel like old news. "What about having my ovaries removed? I was told in the US that around forty to forty-five years old was the recommendation."

"I don't think that is necessary."

Huh. Why do I feel like I'm pleading for him to understand? I switch gears.

"Well, I have a heavy period—that seems to be getting worse as time goes on—so if I had my ovaries removed, it could be a win-win then, yes?"

"Having your ovaries out, you'd still have a period—because you'll still have your uterus."

Okay, he got me on that one. I didn't realize that. I keep going anyway. "So, then, to surgically eliminate a period, I'd have to have a hysterectomy?"

"Correct."

"Would you perform one of those?"

"No, not typically, as it is a larger surgery and takes longer to get approved if you go the public route. I operate privately, too, of course, but it would be an out-of-pocket cost for something I don't feel is necessary."

"Okaaaay." I take a breath as my foot shakes back and forth. I want to find some sort of agreement with him on how best to move forward, and doing nothing isn't computing for me. "So, if I don't do anything surgically, do you recommend I just continue with annual pelvic screenings and blood tests from here on out?"

"Yeah, you can do that...but it really doesn't help *prevent* ovarian cancer. Because, if it is found, it is the kind of cancer where it really is too late to do anything about it."

Oh my gosh. Then why not have my ovaries out?

I'm starting to feel like he isn't at the cutting-edge of his research. Isn't even at the edge of any research.

"And you've really already done all you can do." He is smiling at me, but I only stare in return. "But, if it makes you feel better, then sure, you can organize those annual check-ups through your GP."

Great.

I thank him and leave, hoping I'll never have to drive out to this un-pinpointable location ever again, nor have to schedule any surgeries with this guy.

"Take care and know I'm here for you, whatever you need,"

he adds as I trail out the door.

But this makes me feel even more unsettled. *Why would I need him? He just said I didn't.*

"Maybe this means we should try for a third child, but without the BRCA1 gene?" I ask Mark after we discuss the day's developments, or lack thereof.

He listens patiently as I pace and think, pace and think

"If I am unable to attain a clear direction on what to do with BRCA1," I add, "then I don't feel confident that there will be any promising developments for our BRCA1 child in the future that the gynecologist in Marin thought there would be."

Mark is in easy agreement with this one, seeing me question myself for what, the fourth time? Fifth?

When he doesn't reply to my third-child question, I ask instead, "Would you be okay if I looked into a clinic that works with the lab in the US that built our BRCA1 embryo test?" I sit and take hold of his hands. "I remember coming across an IVF group here—not the one we checked out before but one that might be able to reuse our test."

"Yeah, sure," he acquiesces. He knows that more information will help me move forward—one way or another.

This has really become my prerogative, Imogen. I'm feeling sad inside here. Like I'm losing you. No one is able to help me see over my heavy shoulders, and I am desperate to see.

In my initial consultation, again over Zoom, the doctor at this new-to-us IVF practice tells me, "It is actually strongly discouraged to transfer an embryo with BRCA1 in Australia. Unless it is your only option, which you would have to prove to the government, as well as undergo the extensive required counseling."

What in the world? Why hasn't anyone told me this? The previous IVF doctor? The oncologist?

I need a moment and am grateful I'm hearing this over Zoom instead of in person, so I can tend to my igniting feelings quicker than if my body was in a new space needing to follow social norms. Because not only am I angry—at the rules, at being led on by other doctors—but I am also taking this quite personally. Like a part of me is rejected without a chance to be known.

I quickly regroup and assess these new hoops before me. *Sure, we can undergo counseling,* I think. But if pushed—if someone deliberately asked if I'd be okay knowing I gave my child cancer, or knowing my choice would make *her* have to choose whether or not to have invasive surgeries or risk her own life—I will lose it either in anger or tears.

"Okay." I exhale loudly. "Nobody told us that."

I circle back to our other question, about trying for a female embryo, then, without the gene.

"We can do another round of IVF, no problem, but we cannot select for gender in Australia or even find out the gender," the doctor says. "Even our labs are not privy to those details. It just isn't done for ethical reasons."

Wow.

A double-whammy I did not see coming.

And yet, I persist.

"What if we do another round of IVF and the sample is sent off to the lab in the US, where we built our test before, and *they* give me the gender results?" For a moment, I am pleased with myself.

"No, we can't do that," she quickly states.

Why the fuck not? I want to scream. Why wouldn't Australia be in favor of having a female that doesn't have the gene if they don't want the gene passed on enough to have this regulation in the first place?

I become that irritating, tone-deaf client who pleads her case a few different ways and receives the same response every time: No.

"This is why," she says, "couples sometimes fly out of the country to do IVF."

But the country is still closed.

When I first moved to San Francisco, I didn't have a job. What I had instead was two months' worth of rent money saved, the motivation to hustle, and an inner knowing that this was the place for me.

Years before, while finishing up film school in Boulder, an ad on my computer screen caught my eye. I was emailing off my thesis paper when the banner, for a flight to SF with the Golden Gate Bridge in the background, appeared and I was immediately pulled into other images: dancing to my favorite song as a child, "We Built This City" by Starship, and the opening sequence to *Full House*, dreamily displaying the iconic Painted Ladies in Alamo Square Park. I wanted to follow that pull to San Francisco right then and there, but my father's pragmatism kept me from blindly pitching up jobless in an unknown city.

"You'll end up bagging groceries at King Soopers!" he'd chide.

So, I followed the job offer I already had instead—interning for a producer in Denver—and that job led me to working in LA where I racked up some helpful work experience, but also another call in the form of a dream that I can still remember.

In the dream, I was asleep, cozy in a wood cabin tucked into a misty hillside with a bay of water below. While I slept—with a black cat beside me—a man tended to the garden outside. In the thick, almost England-like fog, he planted things for me. Veggies, bushes, trees. His hands were caked in dirt, his muscles solid and motions fluid. I couldn't place who he was, and we didn't interact, but his presence felt loving and comforting. Like he could hear me without either of us speaking. And when I woke, it brought that pull to San Francisco to the forefront of my mind.

Two years later, I found a way to arrive confidently in that city. It felt like an energetic fit from the moment I inhaled the Northern California air; I just *knew* that abundance, and perhaps that person, would be there. And yet, my mind kept turning over the questions, *Will I be able to find a job?* and *What is next?*

The questions began when I interviewed at Lululemon. The brand was just becoming big—this was 2007—and I wanted to be a part of that blooming energy. What I didn't like and couldn't manifest, no matter how hard I tried, was a *five-year plan.*

"Here is the application form," the perky brunette who'd flown down from Vancouver to run our orientation session said. "Part of our brand is goal-setting. We pride ourselves on helping each other realize our goals."

The applicant to my right put on a big smile and went to work. Her pen was propped in her hand like a magic wand, and she swiped it over those questions with an enthusiasm that was completely absent from me.

First of all, I didn't like the pressure of planning that far ahead, even then. *Why do they need to know what my goals are?* I questioned. *I don't even know what my goals are! I like running but don't want to run a marathon… I like creating but don't want to attach myself to something for the sake of having a goal…*

Second, it felt like they were asking me to carve out a piece of my soul so they could snack on it. As a group! And I wasn't going to hand it over. It sucked out all the fun. All the serendipity.

Beneath their hopeful eyes and rah-rah cheers, I felt trapped.

I got out of there, wished them all well, and wondered, walking back up Steiner Street, *Is something wrong with me?*

I did some journaling later on about what I really wanted: creativity and collaboration. Working with others to make things happen with a togetherness and alignment that feels free.

It wasn't long after penning those thoughts that I was offered a temp job at Pixar through a friend of a friend. *Yes!* I screamed inside every day I was in that environment. Through the position, I had the privilege of working in different offices—a tryout of sorts—to see what each department did and how they all contributed to the company. I spent time with artists and intelligent minds and people wanting to lift one another up in celebration of their talents.

When the temp job was over, a full-time position in production became available. This felt like the mecca for me—and a tipping point for great things to come. I had studied production in school, had experience in it from my time in LA, and the culture aligned with what I wanted from filmmaking.

You have arrived, Lindsay. This is the moment that the plan that society has encouraged all your life has been preparing you for! I thought, walking into my formal interview. And: *Thank goodness I didn't try to force it with Lululemon!*

Sitting across from the producer conducting the interview, I leaned in, engaged, ready.

"You do know this is a five-year commitment, right?" she asked me.

"Yes, I saw that," I said, although not entirely sure it registered until she said it aloud. "But that is great, right, assuming promotions are available from within, and you value hard workers to keep them progressing in the business?"

"No, actually. You must commit to this one position for the

duration of the film. Each one takes five years. During that time, there is no movement, nor is a promotion even considered."

There was that five-year plan staring me in the face again. Literally. My gut was shouting, *Run!!! That is too long! Your youth will be over!!!*

But I ignored that flashing alarm bell and proceeded like it didn't matter to me. I really felt like I had found my people.

She wasn't buying it.

"What I'm hearing," she said, "is that you're a creative person—and that should be cultivated," she encouraged. "We had another woman in this position who left before her five years were up to pursue pottery."

She let that hang in the air between us, and I thought, *Pottery? Cool! I'm not going to pursue pottery.*

"And we're just wary of that happening again," she finished.

I didn't get the position, despite my pleading.

She saw through me—or rather, saw something in me I hadn't yet seen or allowed in myself, but that my insides knew: *Give yourself permission to not know what the future holds, Lindsay, and be okay with that.* Almost a whisper, the touch of a feather, saying, *Trust in that, too.*

By the next month, I was working at a production house where I was not only learning and growing creatively—and in good company—but would also be promoted twice in the next couple of years.

And a year after that, I met Mark.

And a couple of years after that, we got a black cat.

I came to equate my earlier dream as a foreshadowing of this necessary pinnacle in my life—one I longed for, was called to, but could not foresee in a five-year plan.

Mark often reminds me of Steve Jobs's words: "You can only connect the dots looking backward." This is what I remember to celebrate: all these experiences as unpredictable and wonderful and what got me to where I am now—just fine, completely capable, and embracing what is to come, whatever that may be.

So now, here I am in Manly, on some kind of precipice unable to see five years down the road. Not necessarily wanting to— reminding myself I don't like it anyway—but nevertheless trying to tap into that inspiration that can get me to the next best step.

I haven't spoken to myself out loud in a while. I don't do that much anymore. Nor have I had any dreams saturated in abundance. What I do have is the space to go for a run along the beach, where I can have my mind to myself next to the rising sun along an extensive horizon.

This is my favorite weekend treat.

Mark stays in with the boys as I pass the octogenarians at the corner, getting ready in their swim caps and "swimmers" (what the Aussies call swimsuits) to wade out into the water and do the impressive thirty-minute swim around the point to Shelly Beach and back.

On the promenade, my sneakers thump below me on the shared bike path, and I listen to music through my ear pods. I see a friend of ours returning from his morning run, and we high- five in passing, then look at our hands and chuckle, feeling a bit awkward with the touch now that shaking hands is taboo, but wave each other off because we're both in our own worlds and are not strangers.

At the north end of the beach, I do a loop around Queenscliff, and when I head back to the south corner, I take off my shoes and hold them so I can run the last mile feeling the sand between my toes and the occasional cold lap of a receding wave.

The beach faces east and the morning light warms my face.

I want to do this, I hear myself saying. *I am ready.*

A big feeling in me is back and stronger than ever. I feel

radiant, supported by an energy bigger than myself.

The time is now. Now or never.

And I feel infinitely grateful to you, Imogen.

For helping me arrive at this desire and for sticking around in my head and heart. Because who knows? If I didn't know you were there and so much like me in your genetic makeup, I may not have wrestled so intensely for all these years with whether or not to bring you into being.

Without you, I wouldn't have even considered a third child—something I never saw myself wanting or being capable of. Not until I saw those lab results informing me of your potential existence.

When I stop running, I catch my breath and walk—still shoeless, my sneakers tucked under my arms—up the concrete boat ramp to the coffee shop at the lifesaving club. I order two long blacks (like an Americano in the US) for me and Mark.

With full hands warm from the paper cups, I walk the fifty meters back to our apartment and up the slick terracotta tiles to our front door. Then I walk through, set down my shoes, and announce over my shoulder, "All right, I can do it. I want to do it! Let's go!"

"Huh?" Mark asks, as he is mid-negotiation with the boys on who knows what. They all turn to me, thinking we're off on an outing I haven't yet disclosed. *Whoops.*

I shuffle the boys out to the wide balcony where they can kick a soccer ball back and forth. The sun follows me back into the lounge room and dances along the blond wood floor when I hand Mark his coffee.

"I'm ready for another round," I explain.

"Of...?" he asks, picking up dishes from the boys' breakfast.

"Of IVF," I say, following him into the kitchen nook.

"Ohhhh." He laughs, setting down the plates.

I put my hands over his so he doesn't run the water. "It feels

like now is finally the time—because it is the moment we have—
an open window. If we're going to give it another go, we do it
now, and I'm ready for it."

The light is soft, the air coming through the screen cool from
a gentle breeze brought by the shoulder season of fall. It is just
one of those magical days when everything looks more beautiful.
Any conflict the boys have with each other in the background
doesn't penetrate me.

Mark brings his coffee over to the couch and sits down facing
the balcony. I sit down facing him. He catches my eyes. I see his
vulnerability pooling there, along with his worry, fear, and love.
So much love. "I'm ready, too," he tells me.

And it feels *so* good.

That evening, I circle back to Gideon. He is in the bath, which
is full of bubbles, and I'm sitting on the floor, tucked between the
tub and the toilet. I tell him that we're going to try for another
child. "But," I'm sure to caveat, "you might have a baby brother
or sister… We don't know yet."

Either way—a girl like me or a third boy in the family like
Mark—it feels like we're broadening our home base here so far
away from our own parents and siblings, bringing more of our
tribe in to enjoy it with us, experience it with us.

Sometimes it takes a third to find the right balance.

Sometimes life is better left unplanned.

And at all times, it has behooved me to give in to such
callings.

33 | a cacophony

Like *Groundhog Day*, we have to rebuild the test and go through genetic counseling, *again*. At least this time, the counselor presenting the facts is on a Zoom call with me and has a toddler running around in the background, which makes for a more personable session. She skims over the bits that I already know and we share a good laugh, at last.

At the same time, COVID cases increase with the delta variant, and drop-offs become challenging at Julian's preschool. He has a new teacher, and his hesitancy to leave my side becomes a slow, creeping, wet blanket over our happy vibes.

One day after school, while Julian and I watch Gideon in his ninja class, Julian hops off the loveseat we're sharing and points to a red Powerade in a vending machine.

"Mom, can I have one of those drinks?" he asks.

Since it's raining outside and we can't dawdle around like we normally do, I say yes to the added entertainment when I'd normally say no to the sugar and food coloring.

Julian chugs his drink in minutes.

Not such a stretch of entertainment after all, I think, unsurprised when he announces, "I'm busting!" and heads for the toilet.

"Can you come with?" he asks, running ahead.

I grab my bag and follow, closing the narrow door to the restroom behind us. Julian sits on the toilet, and his pee comes out bright red.

Is that dye from his drink? I wonder as my brain tries to catch up with what I'm seeing. And then: *No. That isn't red pee.*

Oh my gosh. Stay calm. Stay calm, I tell myself, realizing it is blood.

"Ahhh!" Julian screams, wide-eyed, seeing the blood, too. "What is happening?"

"I don't know. Does it hurt?" I ask, entirely out of my depth.

"I'm scared."

"Okay, Julsie," I say as he finishes up and the bleeding seems to stop as quickly as it started. My heart thuds and adrenaline surges through me. *What to do? What to do?*

I am in shock, but, like Julian, am scared and want answers. I keep myself steady so I don't scare him more.

"Let's go get Gideon," I tell him. "We'll drive to the doctor to find out what is going on."

When we arrive, Julian is asked to pee in a cup. The dipstick shows there is a faint trace of blood in his urine, but the doctor doesn't want to prescribe antibiotics until the lab results are back.

"Any recent injuries to the area?" the doctor asks, looking at his computer. "It says here an impact wound is the likeliest cause for this kind of thing."

"No...not that I know of," I say, surprised by the diagnosis.

We turn to Julian, and he shakes his head. He is communicative enough at this age, especially when hurt, for me to believe him.

To be thorough, the doctor has us schedule an ultrasound of his kidneys and urinary tract. Given how shaken up I am, he also gives me a referral to a pediatric urologist to follow up with after Julian's scan.

I have a week and a half to go until my ovaries are full enough of follicles that can be extracted, fertilized, and grown to Day 5 or 6 for BRCA1 testing. The state of New South Wales is also slowly closing down again in the background: no interstate travel, work-from-home restrictions, and talk of schools only being open for the children of essential workers.

Julian, meanwhile, is regularly returning home from school with a bag of wet pants and reports of incontinence. I find I am washing clothes more frequently.

"You doing okay, Julian?" I ask him one Wednesday afternoon, in the car on our way to pick up Gideon.

"I don't want to go to school," he says. "When is it the weekend?"

"Just two more days," I tell him, hoping this gives him some comfort.

Julian's ultrasound is a long ordeal, but he is remarkably cooperative and patient. We've seen no more blood, nor any additional symptoms.

The technician is quick to tell us that she doesn't see anything alarming, and the GP follows up with a call indicating the same.

The pediatric urologist tells us something similar.

"Withholding is so common in this age group," she says, "and the urinary tract is connected to constipation as well, so that is very likely the case here."

After all the worry and googling to try and fill-in-the-blanks of what could possibly be happening, this feels anticlimactic.

The next Monday, I have a parent-teacher conference over the phone with Julian's new, older female teacher. I get right to it and ask her why she thinks he is wetting his pants.

"He wasn't listening to me," she says, "so I told him he had to sit out of a game until he was ready to listen. Then he wet himself."

I sigh. That is never easy to hear as a parent and was probably hard for him to experience, too, especially if he was shouted at in front of his friends.

"Hmm, sounds like he is stressed," I offer, looking for empathy and a partner to aid him through this, to help him find comfort in my absence.

"No…I think he might have ADHD…my son does, and he just doesn't listen."

What? This is not what I was expecting, and I feel attacked. *Hmm, probably how Julian feels*, I think next.

I want to generate some compassion toward her and her son, recognizing she is likely strained from her experiences at home, but instead I tune her out. Trying to put a label on Julian is not helpful for me.

I close my eyes and pinch the bridge of my nose to get through the end of our conference. Another discussion I am thankful to not have in person.

As an experiment, I keep Julian home from her classroom on Tuesday and Wednesday. To my surprise, I find that his incontinence must be constipation-related because he has more bowel movements in two days than I could've ever guessed would come out of a four-year-old.

This brings up a lot of sadness for me. I want to help and protect him from this pain and discomfort, but I somehow missed this before.

I question myself, Imogen. *Is it because I'm focused on having a third child? Occupied by all of these separate steps sucking at my attention?*

I shift the entirety of my attention to Julian in this moment. He usually has such an enthusiasm for life—a sweetness in him that he offers up with gusto—that he must really be struggling for these symptoms to be so constant. Seeing him happy at home and not bothered—all while having no accidents—makes it clear to me that this teacher-class combo is no longer working for him.

But I still have appointments to get to in downtown Sydney to measure my follicles and see when I'll be ready for my retrieval.

At our next drop-off, Julian fights going in and cries hysterically when we separate.

I walk to the car wiping away my own tears, feeling like a failure as a mother, and questioning if it is all too much, when a kind teacher we knew from when Gideon was in preschool stops to ask if I am okay.

She gives me a hug.

It doesn't even seem allowed in the current COVID climate—and because I happen to have a bad cold—but I melt into the human connection, appreciating that she sees me and can offer me this comfort when I feel so far away from home.

So far away from where people might've been able to help me before we got to this crescendo.

She assures me she'll call me if Julian needs anything, and I feel rebolstered to get back to my car. I resign myself to seeing this round of IVF through and trusting the hands that Julian is in today.

I drive off into the empty, postapocalyptic streets, thinking about how these stressors seem to be stacking into a barrier—a barrier that is increasing in solidity.

Will I make it through?

In the waiting room at the doctor's office, I try to hold in a cough behind my mask, but it blasts out of my mouth in a cacophony.

Well, that backfired, I think as all the eyes behind the other masks in the room find mine with trepidation.

Behind the exam room door, under a sheet, I lie still while a nurse takes my measurements. No one does much talking, as I track her movements on the monitor. I see her mark the numbers "18" and "20." She wraps the session by telling me that my follicles are close enough to being a mature size, so the coming Monday will be my retrieval day.

Close enough? I step away, wondering, then also thinking, *Where is the doctor? Why am I not hearing this from her?* as I recall previous preretrieval measurements being closer to twenty-two or twenty-four. But no one is around.

This must be the skeleton crew. *People don't want to be here right now*, I think, and keep my mouth shut.

Mark and I go for COVID PCR tests on Saturday—a requirement for the retrieval. We are both so snotty that we can't stop toggling between thoughts: *What will happen if we test positive? Will we lose these eggs and have to reschedule?*

We don't know, and we don't actually want to know. To say we are tense feels like an understatement. We sleep, but not deeply, like the night before an early flight.

The results come through for both of us at 5:00 a.m., stating the same: *Negative for COVID-19.*

I'm in two worlds reading the text: thankful that we can complete the process we've started even though the starting-off point—of how mature my eggs actually are—feels a bit shaky, but also bothered that I have to put Julian back into a stressful environment come Monday to get to the finish line.

34 | a red-hot go

On Monday, I leave the house early, stepping into an Uber with my mask on at 6:00 a.m. to arrive by 6:30 a.m. for my pre-procedure prep. The driver isn't wearing a mask. I text Mark—*Shouldn't he be wearing a mask?!*—and then discreetly roll my window down a crack, thinking, *At this point, with my cold, I'm probably more of an annoyance to him than he is to me.*

I am the only one outside the high-rise building when I arrive. I take a seat on a polished bench in the lobby and wait for someone to unlock the elevator to the tenth floor. A lab tech steps in a few minutes later with a key, greeting me kindly and making small talk.

The others must've come up through a back entrance, I think, trying not to show my discomfort over being the first one here. We ride up together and exchange a few smiles in silence. I wonder— while I hold in another cough—if he will be the one receiving my most precious insides in a couple of hours for testing and safekeeping.

Once I've checked in, I'm led to a small room to sit down behind an opaque glass door. *This is different,* I think, *being kept in a holding area.* I hang tight, though, filling the empty bin next to me with a growing pile of tissues.

My phone pings with a text from Mark that Julian made it into his classroom okay, with minimal resistance. I release a long sigh.

Mark then tells me he is on his way.

Before the retrieval, Mark and I each take one more COVID test. The results are instantly negative, so we can proceed. My upper respiratory symptoms are so bad, though, that the anesthesiologist tells me afterward, laughing, that he had to keep a constant suction going at the back of my throat for my "secretions"—so I could breathe.

Um, gross.

Once I'm fully awake, the embryologist tells me that I have a solid egg count of about seventeen, but not all of them are mature. Heck, I am nearly thirty-eight, so I'm not alarmed or put out by this news. I'm just elated that it's all over with and I can get dressed, collect our boys, and recover from this cold.

That afternoon, we learn that six of my eggs successfully fertilized. The head embryologist adds that he isn't super confident with their quality but assures me he'll touch base on Day 3 as to how the embryos are maturing.

Okay, I think, *we're still in the running here.*

Six is still a solid starting point and, recalling my IVF doc's words in SF, half will likely make it to Day 5/6 and of those, another half will likely be BRCA1-free. *Very similar,* I mentally match, *to our previous experience.*

The next day, New South Wales goes into another full lockdown due to a spike in COVID cases.

On Day 3, the embryologist calls to tell me, "Unfortunately, only two embryos are still dividing and they're not looking great. But we'll keep watching them, and I'll call you on Day 5 with the next report."

Not looking great is never good, but still not a definite answer, I tell myself.

I share the news with Mark.

We still have hope for one. All we need (and want) is one.

On Day 5, one embryo is left standing.

"We're going to give it to Day 6 to see if it divides some more before we test it," the embryologist says. "It's not in the best shape, but maybe it will look better tomorrow, and we'll test a sample then. We have the test here in our lab, so we will be able to give you the results with our call tomorrow."

Oh, wow, that is soon, I think as my heart rate increases and my mind catches up with the timing and these new details.

I notice that I still feel okay. I am still hopeful.

Day 6 is warm and bright.

The boys are in the driveway doing laps on their scooters, taking turns sticking out a foot or an arm, and calling me "poo" as they pass by. *To laugh or not to laugh?* Mark and I snicker silently to each other.

We are sitting in camping chairs watching them, having a jovial distanced conversation with our neighbor over our shared fence. We're comparing notes and checking in, after hearing him lose it earlier with his four-year-old.

"All okay?"

"Yes, I was just screaming because my child snuck out the window and ran down the street without telling us," he says, his hand cradling his forehead, "and we couldn't find him…"

"Oh my gosh," I say, and think, *The panic!* I start to continue, "Makes sense…" when my phone rings.

Mark takes over the conversation, while I step into the garage.

"This is Lindsay," I answer.

It's the lab. "Hi, Lindsay," the embryologist says, "I have some disappointing news…"

Ugh. My heart freezes, suspended in time.

"The Day 6 sample tested positive for BRCA1 and is chromosomally abnormal."

A double punch.

I feel my heart pound as I blow out my breath.

"Your doctor will call to follow up with you."

I thank him.

"Take care and stay safe," he says—the sign-off of the times. "I hope we get to work with you again soon."

But I know this will not be the case.

This was our Hail Mary. I don't have another retrieval in me. I know it in my bones. I don't want to do it.

The river of life is surging ahead at full force—COVID, kids, feelings, ailments, unknowns—and doing this round felt like fighting that flow already.

Maybe it's time, Lindsay, I hear my inner voice say. *Time to surrender fully*.

I walk out of the garage, emptied by reality. I have no tears, no overwhelming disappointment—only a knowledge that the space we were fighting for, longing for, desperate to try on for size, is not available to us. The window has shut and locked.

I'm sad to deliver the news to Mark and, eventually, the boys.

But strangely, I am also okay. I am okay because I said *yes* to the experience of trying. I gave it *a red-hot go*—as one of Gideon's teachers once said—and I can now stop digging in myself for more reserves that may or may not be there.

We speak to our doctor that afternoon.

"Guys, I anticipate us reaching your ideal outcome after three tries. At your age, we just have to expand our options for success," she says.

That might have been nice to hear before our retrieval, I think, but it doesn't matter now anyway. We're not as determined for those options. We've had success and are blessed with hands and hearts that are full.

"Thank you, but we really just had this one in us and don't have the bandwidth for another round," we tell her.

"Okay. I'm here if you change your mind."

This time turns out to be New South Wales' longest and most restrictive lockdown yet, going into three months. Children in all schools are expected to stay home and do home learning. Masks are mandated, many shops are forced to close, and gatherings of any size are no longer an available respite for us.

I host jumping-off-the-bed contests, dance parties, and count how many forward-rolls the boys can do up and down the hall in one go. I try everything I can to keep their volume down, physicality up, and my patience in check. There are tears and meltdowns—from Gideon and I both—getting through his writing homework for year 1. Julian is beside himself with joy for not having to go to school, and Mark keeps having to mute himself on Zoom calls for work because of all the ruckus the boys make in the background. It really is mania.

After the boys are in bed one night, I say to Mark, "I think it's time."

"Time for what?" he cuts me off, exasperated. "You've gotta stop being cryptic like that with me. I cannot read your mind!"

"Let me finish."

He stops and lets me continue.

"I think it's time to release our BRCA1 female embryo," I breathe out. "I'm exhausted and I think that—this all working out this way," I gesture in big circles with my hands, "is a blessing in disguise, because no way could I handle this level of intensity and be pregnant right now…"

He looks at me, lifting his eyebrows in question. But, no, I'm not quite finished.

"Much less have a baby and be 'on it' with his or her needs and have anything left for our boys. Even if we changed the way we thought about raising our children and could find full-time help, I wouldn't be participating in the way I want to."

I sigh again. This is not easy to realize and honor, but there it is, Imogen. The truth.

Mark hears me. He knows it, too, in himself. Even though we wish it wasn't true sometimes, that doesn't make it less true.

"It's like that facilitator told us dads at that men's circle in Marin: Wanting another child and having the capacity for another child are two separate things," Mark says.

"I get that now."

"And would you say yes to a gestational carrier if that were an option for us?"

"No." I pause, knowing this is a fantastic option for some but would not take away the magnitude of what would fall into my hands after the birth. "I wouldn't."

"I just want to check. Make sure we've really discussed all the possibilities here," Mark says, no longer wanting to be on the receiving end of my ping-ponging feelings.

"I appreciate that," I say. "But I'm feeling solid on the big-picture stuff. It's no longer just about IVF and BRCA1 and pregnancy. It's about parenting beyond having a baby, too, and being available for the beautiful, growing children that we have in our ever-evolving circumstances."

"Yup."

Mark wraps his arm around me, and I bury my head into his shoulder, letting these words sink in.

I do the hard thing next, to finalize our decision.

Action helps me. Clean the room, remake the space, tidy up. Marie-Kondo my life for magic to appear.

There is still magic here, right? There's gotta be, Imogen. There's gotta be. I mean, I'm here speaking to you and there is magic in that. Something that exceeds the physical, the tangible, the knowable. And that is the definition of magic, is it not?

Sunlight glimmers on the sea in bright fractures when I call our IVF clinic in San Francisco from our balcony. Too intense to stare at, too difficult to see directly, leaving only blinding impressions, but warm and encompassing all the same.

When my doctor's nurse answers, I tell her we'd like to sign the necessary paperwork to no longer store our embryo with the BRCA1 gene. I admit I'm not 100 percent sure about it—nor probably ever will be—but that doing so will help us move forward. Help me move forward.

I close my eyes as I release these words. When I reopen them, I turn my head back toward our home.

"Well, we never really throw anything away," the nurse reveals.

"Don't tell me that!" I say, setting my sight again to the sun's glare. I'm partly relieved, partly frustrated—but, most of all, grateful she doesn't blatantly tell me that I'm discarding you.

There are no other emotions tagging along this day. Suddenly no longer tethered to IVF and embryos, I float through the motion of stepping inside, off our balcony, and away from the burning color.

"We'll set up a Zoom call to notarize both of your signatures.

Have your IDs ready; a passport is fine."

It isn't long until it's done.

At some point thereafter—either in the bath or in the car—I tell the boys, "We tried, but we aren't going to have another baby, after all."

One of them might've asked, "But why, Mommy?"

And I fight a catch in my breath to say, "Ah, it just didn't work out."

And they go back to splashing their toys or looking out the window to the ocean, and we continue living.

part III | *after* you

35 | fill-in-my-own-blank

When we emerge out of lockdown months later, we're all like plants perking back up with water and sunshine. Everyone feels a need for expansion and change.

It is slowly revealed that one of our favorite families, with two boys and a lot of parenting overlap in terms of awareness and humor, bought a place in Newcastle, a few hours up the coast. They've been too boxed in by their apartment and want the space to peel away the layers of stress that the last couple of years piled onto them.

I want that, too, I think, when I hear the news, already anticipating the loss of not having their presence in our lives.

Then, our fun-loving, loud, and lovely neighbors over the fence beside us announce that they, too, are moving about thirty minutes away, up to Newport, also for more space and no shared walls. Their sentiment is *It's been grand, could be a big mistake, but see ya!* and off they go; we haven't seen them since.

Maybe jumping on this bandwagon is just what I need, I think. *Just what our family needs.* And I fill-in-my-own-blank with what, exactly, that need could be: a commitment to Australia.

A lot of thoughts fight for the space I now have since releasing you, Imogen.

These are the loudest, brought on by the energy in our surroundings: *Here we are. The country is still closed to international travel. Maybe now it's time to* really *see if this is the place for us. Perhaps I wasn't looking at living here the "right" way before? Because in the back of my mind, we were always going to return to the US…*

Yes, that is where I settle in, as a foundation to build upon. That is where a motion begins that I conduct.

"We won't know unless we try!" I tell Mark, whose favorite apartment is the one we're in now, the one that was our much-loved Airbnb, steps away from the ocean. "Maybe we can have a place to make our own, though! Where the energy feels like ours." I continue to cite any little thing to help my case. "This spot is so damp up against the cliff here, with cockroaches and spiders in summer, and I bang my elbows on the walls every time I use the loo…"

A week-ish later, a money-hungry agent comes knocking.

"If you guys ever want to move out, I'd really love to take over your lease—make this place a corporate rental," he says. *Hmm, interesting.*

He knocks a few more times. Gets our numbers, texts us. Becomes borderline irritating. (In case it isn't obvious, Imogen, this guy is not Australian but American.)

We hear of another family in Gideon's class that is moving for more space and a backyard—literal greener pastures.

The momentum is infectious. So much so that Mark wonders, too, what is out there? Could we really live here, buy something and put down roots?

Could Australia fill this space in me? In us?

We come across a spot on the Eastern Hill of Manly, tucked away from the busyness, facing the Harbour side. It is a top-floor unit with carpet—presumably helpful for combating our new habit of noisiness—and stunning views of the ferries coming and going. The Balgowlah Heights hills are visible from the balcony, plus a smidge of the Headlands, reminiscent of Mila's Angel Island view in Marin.

"I think this is it," I whisper to Mark, feeling a connection to the space a few steps in. The unit is sunny and bright and has AC.

"Let's think about it," he whispers back, keen for the agents not to overhear us.

"The space is larger than it looks online," I say to an older lady also moving through the rooms, unable to contain myself. She doesn't hear me though, or think I'm talking to her, and just walks on. We later learn she lives across the hall.

Back outside the unit, we discover it comes with two lock-up garage spaces and access to a shared grass-filled back garden with a separate, enclosed pool.

"Moving quickly makes me nervous," Mark tells me when we walk back down the hill to reengage with the day.

But I'm already feeling like the space is ours. I want to make this decision hesitation-free, take a bold leap, and see it all happen. Hitting this shield around Mark, though, I decide to hold my tongue awhile, letting him come around if he wants to—all while a bigness inside me expands.

By the afternoon, Mark is caught up in an enthusiasm for the unit, too, and feels motivated to make an offer.

"It's not like we're going to the US in the foreseeable future," he says.

I nod with a secret smile.

After a few back-and-forths, the offer is accepted.

Whoa! That was fast! I think, feeling about to burst with excitement. *Maybe it's a message from the universe that this is where we're meant to be!*

We sign some paperwork, put down a deposit, and the market deems it sold.

Our new rhythms and routines soon start to take shape. Mark walks to a coworking space next to the beach most mornings, dropping Gideon at school along the way. It's a nice twenty minutes where they get to greet other families that they now see walking to school, too, living on this side of Manly.

Julian is in a new-to-us Montessori school a short drive away (no bridges), with a five-mornings-a-week schedule. We said yes when a spot appeared after the latest lockdown, hoping the familiarity with the environment would be a fresh opportunity for him to reacclimate to a classroom.

New tenants move in a couple of floors below us, and we quickly befriend them. The family has a daughter Julian's age, and it isn't long until she joins us in after-school scootering and biking activities in the building's cul-de-sac beside the garages. Along with a nine-year-old boy who lives downstairs, we develop a new at-home play group.

On the last day of the school year, mid-December, one of the building's tenants organizes to keep a neighbor's large, rectangular trampoline in our shared back garden while she sells her house. The boys rejoice in its presence, feeling like Christmas came early.

To me, home ownership in an apartment doesn't get much better than this with a shared happiness-inducing community and activities for the kids. I feel like we've hit the jackpot.

Mark, however, starts to home in on the building's extractor fan. It is right next to our unit and makes a noise like the hum of a plane engine. I brush it off, too distracted and delighted by all the recent happiness, so I am surprised when Mark, irritated by the fan and now the wind hitting our single-pane windows at this high northwest-facing location, proclaims, "It feels like I'm living in a tent. I give this place twelve months, tops!"

The next day, as I pull into the apartment complex with some groceries, I spot one of our neighbors nearby, tinkering with his moped while his small dog looks on, keeping him company. He spots me, too, and I lift my hand to wave.

I lock the car and am stepping out of our garage when I hear, "That wasn't right, you know!"

I turn and he's standing right beside me with an expectant look on his face.

"What was that?" I ask, trying to mask my surprise at his nearness and tone.

"Putting that trampoline in our backyard! It blocks our view—and we weren't asked! That is not the way it is done. Just so you know," he adds sourly.

Sheesh, such a grump, my thoughts quickly turn.

I don't have much to say other than, "Well, the kids really like it?" Then I walk away to get my bags upstairs.

A couple of hours later, Mark and the neighbor who told us about the trampoline in the first place move the trampoline closer to the fence so that the other guy's view isn't blocked. Yet, *I* get cornered by his wife later, desperate to have her plea of "the injustice of it all" heard.

You're barking up the wrong tree, lady, I think, surprised that this woman—who told me when we moved in that she is a substitute teacher of young kids—doesn't get it.

The thrill I felt from our move-in experience slowly disintegrates.

By the end of December 2021, Australia opens back up for international travel. After nearly two years of the country being closed, this is massive news. An inner desperation in me is triggered: to fly home, now knowing that we actually *can*. But the inflated costs and chaos surrounding travel keep me focused on enjoying the benefits of our new home instead.

I tell myself, *How lucky are we to spend this summer using our new shared pool—and the trampoline, while it lasts.*

The first few weeks of the 2022 school year, Julian starts fighting me when leaving the house. He does not want to go to school, and I fluctuate between calmness and sheer will to get him down the four flights of stairs, into the car, and buckled.

We always get to school on time, but when we arrive, Julian often takes off running down the sidewalk in the opposite direction of the school gate, out of sight. One day, the only way I can get him back to the gate is by picking him up while he kicks, screams, and then bites into my shoulder.

What. Is. Going. Onnnn? I wonder, cycling through possible reasons in my mind as I grit my teeth to the pain, holding a look of *Nothing to see here!* on my face to get us back to the entry.

"Good morning, Lily," the head of school pleasantly greets one of the children, now lined up in front of us. "Good morning, Molly," she says to the next one, sharing a smile.

How lovely, I think, as Julian pulls himself together in front of his peers, wondering why he was running away from this.

"Hello, Julian," the head of school then says coldly, with a grimace, holding him in her gaze.

Wait, huh? I think, clocking the difference as he limply shakes her hand.

I give him a wave and say behind him, "Have a great day, Jules, love you!" being sure to watch as he makes his way inside. He doesn't turn around to see me, but the head of school stops me before I leave.

"Julian doesn't listen to me. You need to tell him to listen to me!" she says with such severity that I'm caught off guard.

Her face turns foul in my wordless reply. I want to defend him but am put off by her energy.

Here we go again with another bad-tempered teacher, I think as my heart sinks and I mumble a promise to talk to him, making a mental note to be more compassionate than reprimanding when I do.

I get in my car and shut the door, buckling up.

It takes a few long breaths, after a flood of feelings, before I'm actually able to drive back into Manly.

A few days later, it starts to rain nonstop.

For weeks upon weeks.

"We've had the fire, famine—and now the flood!" people say, laughing.

But I don't find it funny.

Roads, fields, and play areas become so waterlogged that we are confined indoors after school and on weekends, being our noisy selves for all to hear.

The neighbors below us say, "Oh, we get it—you have floorboards, right?" They think there is so much noise because we don't have the buffer of carpet between our floor and their ceiling—but, sigh. This is not the case. Our unit is fully carpeted. Boys are just loud.

This underlying hum of stress intensifies within me when the building's extractor fan is actually broken and takes ages to fix because of the rain. Our neighbors knock on our door (some even at 6:30 a.m., like the old lady's daughter from across the hall) when leaks appear in their own apartments because of the fan repair.

We're the messengers, not the handyman, people! I want to shout, becoming the outlandish one.

We then learn that a friend of ours' wife—my age—is dying from cancer in the US. *Fuck.* It is awful, and I become keenly aware that we're unable to be there to hold him or his son, who is between our boys' ages. We say to come and visit when they can, but at the same time, I wonder, *How? How are we going to accommodate them in this pressure cooker?* Then I think, too, that maybe they won't be bothered. Maybe all of this stuff is just noise that doesn't matter and will work itself out.

And yet, my boiling point comes when Julian's teacher emails me to meet with her one-on-one. When I sit across from her, rather than focusing on his well-being, she points out the imperfections in how he writes his letters.

His letters, Imogen! That he is just learning. At four years old. After months of lockdown.

"I think he has a learning delay," she says.

Oh. My. Fucking goodness, I seethe.

A few nights later, I finish Jodi Picoult's latest release, *Wish You Were Here*, about the pandemic and a trip to the Galapagos Islands.

I can't say more because it would ruin the book, but suffice it to say, I can't fall asleep. The story is supercharging my brain, and I feel like I'm lying in an alternate reality, and my real life is going on somewhere else without me.

Mark is already passed out, so I walk through the dark, quiet house to the living room and tuck my knees into my chest on the couch.

Outside the window, the lights of the homes surrounding the bay reflect off the water and ripple onto the living room floor in front of me.

This feels like the first time I've stopped in days. Months.

The first time I've noticed any sort of beauty.

And yet, it doesn't sink in as real.

A steady stream of saline coats my face as I take in the glow of passing ferry boats.

Why am I crying so hard? I think, unable to turn off the tears.

My breathing hitches as I start to calm down.

All that appears is a knowingness inside that I am too far away from my family, too far away from anything familiar, and too far away from a bosom friend who could tell me, *You're all right, this is not normal, it's okay to feel this way.*

The next morning, I press Mark to fly back to San Francisco and Colorado for a visit. But we cannot, yet. His parents arrive next month from South Africa and the visa they needed just came through.

So, we book a flight to the US for three weeks at the end of June, into July. We'll land in Colorado to spend the majority of our stay among family and take a long weekend in SF to see our friends. I sink into this knowledge, feeling like there is a light at the end of this tunnel—a big, cushy pillow waiting for me to lie on and release all that I've been holding.

Colorado. Everything will be okay when we get to Colorado, I keep thinking.

This thought becomes my talisman.

During Mark's parents' stay, my mom calls one morning at an earlier than usual time. She tells me that my aunt, her oldest sister, had a stroke and was flown by helicopter to a hospital.

"She was declining already, losing her sight, and feeling quite nervous about losing her own independence," my mom explains, "and I think on some higher level this is her way of bowing out on her terms…"

This news feels like another heavy dose of reality that I've missed being there for those I care about most and have known the longest.

She continues, "It is only a matter of time, honey. I'm driving to the hospital now. It could be days or hours."

I start to cry.

"I know. I wish you were here," she tells me.

I hang up and feel sad that I haven't seen her since our last visit in April 2019. I'm grateful we've kept in touch with a few letters and text messages but know, too, there wasn't much else I could do with my hands full here, adapting, and our limited overlap in phone call times.

When my mom and I speak again the next day, she tells me my aunt passed away early that morning. Her daughter got to be at her side right before, and though she was unconscious, it was like she held on so my cousin could say goodbye.

"The family is all going to come together for her memorial service...which may be a month or so away, so everyone can make it. I sure hope it is when you are here and you can be a part of it."

"Thanks, Mom. Me, too."

That evening, Mark's parents, the boys, and I, walk to Little Manly Beach to kick the soccer ball around before it gets dark. I tell them about my aunt and they are kind to listen and ask questions.

We see a magnificent sunset—bright splashes of peach and pink and purple across the sky. Though it is stunning, all that settles in me is a feeling of how far away I am from home.

Our flight is now days away. Air travel restrictions have lessened, and Mark's parents returned home safely and COVID-free. At Gideon's school pick-up, I tell some other parents that we'll finally be going home after all this time.

"Make sure you come back!" one mom says.

"Haha, yes, we'll be back," I say.

And as the days go on and we pack our one suitcase for our not-long-enough trip, we hear that sentiment more and more. Not *We'll miss you* or *Enjoy yourselves*, but *Be sure to return to us!*

I let these words fade to the background as an inner peace continues to bloom within me anytime I visualize Colorado. I consider bringing a few extra books I haven't read yet *just in case* we stay a bit longer, but then I set them aside to keep our bags light.

I just want to get there already.

The plane for our long-haul flight is small and packed. The boys are restless. We don't get much sleep. After a connection through San Francisco, where we have to get through a very long domestic security line and then kill hours of time, we are down a few brain cells and up a few meltdowns. On our last leg into Denver, we finally sleep.

We miss my aunt's memorial service by a day. But my mom's other sister is also passing through DIA when we land, on her way back home, and as we step off the escalators at baggage claim, I see my aunt, my mom, and my dad waiting for us. When I lock eyes with all of them, my vison blurs and my chest aches. I'm exhausted. Everyone looks so much older. So much has happened.

We hug. Hard. It feels good to hold one another—like I've met up with my other life that has been happening simultaneously—and I don't want to let go.

It quickly catches up to me that this is a decisive visit—one in which we will have to reevaluate not only *if* we will ever live in Colorado, but when.

Mark is much more hesitant than I am on saying yes to another big move. For so many understandable reasons, but the most prominent one being that he's never not lived near the sea, never been landlocked, never had a snowy winter. When I realize this, Imogen, a new idea arises within me to show him that it will be fine here.

That I need it to be fine.

Even if I don't really know how desperately yet.

I reach out to an admissions director of a local school that I've been loosely in contact with, asking her if there are any South African families in their community I could speak to. *Maybe they can help Mark understand*, I think.

While waiting for her reply, I also ping a mom from Gideon's soccer team back in Australia who I know has a sister in Boulder, to see if she can put me in touch with any South Africans here as well. "Just to help us with some decisions we're making," I share.

Incredibly, within twenty-four hours, I have multiple responses:

"Yes, we do actually have one family at the school," the admissions director tells me. "The mom is American, and the dad is South African!"

And from the soccer team mom: "Of course, my sister would be happy for you to reach out—her best friend is South African!"

Not two days later, we have two meet-ups planned. One for a drink in Boulder to connect with the family from the school. The other, a Fourth of July lunch at the sister's best friend's house.

Imogen, what are the odds? It feels so easy that I'm left wondering, *Was it you who set this up to help your dad? To help* me?

Our first get-together is at an outdoor brewery, with wooden barrel tables scattered around a lawn near a lake. Mark and I order a drink, then lean around a barrel while we wait for the couple to arrive.

"Do you know any South Africans with his last name?" I ask Mark of the guy we're about to meet.

"I did my chartered accountancy articles in South Africa with a guy who had the same last name. I know he was in Colorado years ago but has since moved back to Cape Town. Maybe they know each other?"

Just then, the couple walks up and introduces themselves. We're all in a jolly mood to have found each other, with our rare-seeming similarity.

Right away, Mark asks the husband if he knows of the one guy he worked with before with the same last name, saying they actually resemble one another.

"Of course I know him!" he says and laughs. "He's my

brother!"

"No way!" we exclaim, but our new friend continues.

"And he happens to be right over there!" He smiles and points to a guy across the way, sitting outside the very same brewery.

"Whaaat!" I say.

Mark shakes his head. "I can't believe it."

"He just moved back here at the end of last year. His wife is from Denver, and they have two girls," the brother says.

This is too much fun!

Mark walks over to stand in front of his old friend. It's been nearly twenty years. He asks, "Do you know who I am?"

The guy's stoic face breaks into a wide grin. "Mark Bartels!"

It's an incredible feeling, seeing my South African husband reconnect with a friend from South Africa—in Colorado—both with family here.

I find myself tearing up.

Maybe we can bridge this gap, I think.

We end up eating dinner together and sharing stories, finally in a currency that feels familiar, all while our children are with their grandparents. We leave with a plan to meet again, with the kids, in a couple of days.

The next get-together is our lunch date with the soccer mom's sister's South African friend on her back deck facing the foothills. She hosts us, along with another close South African friend of hers, while they both serve us separate perspectives of their time in Boulder.

It feels like tapping into a long-lost friend-family. We are overwhelmed by their incredible generosity in helping us fill in some blanks—from having family back in South Africa and maintaining those connections, to navigating the winter and finding their people here.

On our drive back to my parents' place, where the boys are

again being looked after, living in Colorado starts to feel doable.

For our long weekend in San Francisco, the boys end up staying back in the open and willing arms of my parents, sister, and their cousins. This is so unexpectedly helpful, allowing us to have heart-to-hearts with those nearest and dearest to us—those I met with Mark and who were by my side during chemo.

"What do you think about us moving back?" I ask; we ask.

Among our favorite haunts—on walks to and from the Golden Gate Bridge, under the Redwood trees in Mill Valley, sitting side by side on Mila's deck—they share their enthusiasm for our return. Most of them encourage us to make it sooner rather than later.

Even if we're in Colorado and not SF, they say, we'd be able to make quick trips back and forth and at least be able to speak on the phone during commute times again. There are so fewer barriers without an ocean between us.

We are missed, Imogen!

"The kids will adjust!" they say, over and over again.

Mark and I leave California with a plan, united in our vision: I will stay in Colorado with the boys. We'll see out the summer spending time with family and looking for a home, while taking up the extra space so graciously offered to us at my parents' place. I'll enroll the boys in school so they can begin in August, with everyone else. Mark will return to Australia. He'll work it out with his team to operate remotely in the US, put our house on the market, and pack up the belongings that we want to keep, selling or donating the rest.

This all makes me incredibly giddy.

We know it is a tall order and will be harder to do apart than together, but we also know it is the easiest and best way for the boys—out of sight, out of mind—staying with the good thing we have going.

The boys take the news surprisingly well, voicing feelings they, too, have buried:

"My teacher doesn't like me," Julian says, "and I don't want to go back there."

"Yes, I can see that," I say, validating him, "and I'm glad I no longer need you to be there, either."

"And I'm happy not to be in the same class anymore as [this one kid]," Gideon piles on. "He just wasn't nice to me, and I didn't know what to do."

"Well, I'm happy for you for that reason then, too."

This reconvening of friends and family becomes more than a pillow for me but a whole space. Here I can fall, with abandon, from the heights we've climbed, knowing there is a wide, comfortable safety net in place, happy and willing to receive us.

Six or so months later, by early 2023, we're all functioning in a kind of flow state where we lose track of the hours. *When have I last felt this way?* I can't even recall.

We have settled into a spacious house with a backyard and within walking distance to my parents' place. Mark has a new routine working from home, with morning swims at an indoor pool nearby and afternoon walk-and-talks, on the phone, around the neighborhood. We get a puppy. And a trampoline.

The boys slot right in with their new school, comfortable among their peers and teachers in ways I haven't seen in years. *Maybe it's because they're finally near those who love us unconditionally,* I think, watching them expand and soar.

Old friends stay with us and visit with their children during the snowy months. The boys sled, build snowmen, make snow angels.

And I finally feel like I have the time and space to see the remainder of this journey through. *Do the US doctors still advise removing my ovaries?* I wonder. I am turning forty this year, after all. And I want to stick around for this!

It's time to find out.

Come April, I have an appointment with an oncological surgeon who is a fellow at UC Health and specializes in BRCA care.

I actually feel excitement building in me through the hour-plus of traffic, driving to her office. It feels like a moment I didn't know I'd been waiting for all these years.

The hospital she works at is under construction, so it takes me another twenty minutes to find parking, and then an additional ten to find the correct entry into the building. Once inside, I look around and realize, *This is where I went for that second opinion my dad insisted on nearly fourteen years ago.*

When my name is called, I'm led down a long corridor. We turn another corner, then another. After a nurse gets my vitals and we commiserate on parking woes, a young, put-together, and assertive woman enters. She introduces herself as the physician assistant (PA).

The PA quickly explains that I will not be seeing the doctor I made my appointment with today because of a family emergency. "Her partner, who you'll meet with instead, is equally as knowledgeable and fantastic. I operate with her all the time."

"Great." I nod, a smidge put off, but thankful for the swift solution and endorsement.

"This is the beauty of having a practice of fellows," she continues. "We can have each other's backs in times like this. The doctor you're seeing today has double the patients, so I'll be taking your history. What brings you in today? It says here you're a BRCA carrier."

Thank you for reading your paperwork, I think, satisfied, before I reply, "Yes, I'm here to see when she recommends me having my ovaries removed—or, if at all—as prevention for ovarian cancer."

We chat some more as she takes notes and then says, "The doctor *will* have an answer for you. She'll be in shortly," and leaves the room.

Thank goodness I'm back in the land of answers!

When the doctor appears and introduces herself, she, wonderfully, has read through my history, and—like a knowledgeable and comforting best friend—dives right in. I feel like we've met before, that is how at ease I am. She has an incredibly disarming bedside manner.

"Our latest research shows that as soon as patients with BRCA1 hit forty, the risk goes up exponentially for ovarian cancer." She pulls up a chart indicating as much so I can follow along. "So, yes, I'd recommend surgery sooner than later."

"I see."

"There is also a slight increased chance for a really bad uterine cancer that, if detected, is impossible to stop."

"Well, I did wonder about a hysterectomy rather than just having my ovaries removed." I pause and then bring up my heavy, uncomfortable, and inconvenient periods that only seem to amplify with age. "I would very much love to not have those anymore."

"We can do that," she quickly replies, unbothered. Undeterred. "It will allow us wider margins for pathology—to make sure there are no cancerous cells already there."

Oh, wow, that was an easy yes.

"We'd remove the cervix, too," she continues, "eliminating any further need for cervical cancer screenings, and also test the tissue there. I'd just have to document your heavy periods so that the cost is covered by your insurance."

"Amazing." Someone is finally meeting me where I am at.

Like is begetting like here, Imogen, and the unfolding is beautiful for me. Her confidence ignites my own. This is what I want. What I've wanted to want but didn't feel I could want out loud. Now I can.

"Thanks," I say. "That is the direction I'd like to go."

The thoughts—*I don't want to think about these things anymore or worry about the what-ifs of my safety!*—emerge from hidden depths within me. Maybe I didn't even give myself the permission to know they were there until this doctor gave me her confidence, unwaveringly.

"Great. Let me look at the schedule and see what is available," she says, plucking away at her keyboard. "Would you be open to coming to our clinic at the Highlands Ranch location? The facilities there are newer, smaller, and the parking is a lot easier."

"Ha! Definitely. You had me at easy parking!"

"Wonderful. Well, I see here I have an 8 a.m. start in two weeks and can do the surgery for you there, then."

"Wow, that is soon!" I can't help but share my surprise. "How is it that you have an opening? It seems whenever I schedule things lately, appointments are months out."

"Well, cancer patients take precedence and I'm doing the scheduling, so I can get you in."

My heart rate increases. *Can I agree to it? Am I ready? Will I have help?*

Yes, yes, and yes.

"Goodness. That is quick, but I would actually like to get it done. My kids are in school through the end of May and my husband isn't traveling…" I think out loud, then take a breath. *Come on, Lindsay,* I tell myself. "Okay, let's do it," I breathe out, then ask, "but, if for some reason, the date doesn't work for my family, would it be possible to reschedule?"

"Of course. You can reschedule up to forty-eight hours in advance."

"Fantastic, thanks."

"Great, I'll book you in," she says. Then she adds, "It is an outpatient surgery, same day. You'll be able to go home that afternoon. We'll get the pathology results the next day as well."

Oof. Yes. Pathology.

There is so much talk of pathology.

Since I've had clear pelvic ultrasounds and clear blood tests up until now, I hadn't thought of needing pathology. This very realistic part of the process harrows me, and I know this surgery needs to be done, no question.

Imogen, I am glad, again, that you don't have to wear these shoes—that you don't have to make these choices.

When the PA reenters to provide expectations for the recovery, my new doc excuses herself, promising to see me soon.

"The recovery is typically four to six weeks, and it is imperative during that time you do not lift anything over ten pounds," the PA says.

"Okay…"

"Because there will be stitching at the top of the vagina." She shows me a handy diagram of the uterus and pelvic anatomy. "Once we remove the ovaries and uterus, we'll bring them through the vagina…" *Eee, too many details!?* "And then sew it up here at the top so none of your bowels or other organs fall through."

"Gosh!" That is quite alarming.

"So, yeah, no lifting heavy objects, okay? Even grocery bags. You'll need help so those stitches don't burst!"

"Got it," I confirm with a nod, trying to reel in my startled expression.

It's a lot to digest, but I leave returning to that energized feeling I had driving down here. I have found the professionals who confidently do these types of surgeries every day and am in the land of family who can support me to get it done.

When I fill my people in on the plan, the support I need is there; it's only when I call an old friend—the one who took such amazing notes for me at my pre-chemo oncology appointment years ago—that I come across something unexpected:

"Maybe you should talk to the shaman?" she suggests.

When the shaman and I speak over Zoom, I take notes—something I don't normally get to do when sitting in a room across from him. And when I share my enthusiasm about what is coming, he shifts my focus.

"I encourage you to mourn the loss of your womb," he says, "and recognize this as a literal removal of a body part that holds so much significance…"

Oh, I didn't think of it that way.

I check inward. Do I feel an upcoming sense of loss right now? *No.* I wonder if that will change.

He goes on to share a concept of time with me in which the three dimensions—past, present, and future—all happen simultaneously.

"If you remove one of the dimensions," he says, "reality would be warped. Therefore, time, as we see it now—linearly—*is* warped, because we don't include the future state."

Interesting, I think, as I scribble that onto paper and circle *warped*.

"The past is the only certainty. Including the future state in the now, in which things will all work out, is for the *best*—but it is hard to square this truth with rational thinking."

I don't quite follow. It feels a bit like mental gymnastics. I look up with my pen poised, ready for him to continue. Then I face the screen again as he does.

"The future is the best possible state because everything is evolved there—unimaginably great—because there is no limit."

That does sound nice…

"So, you must navigate circumstances with compassion in unity of all these paradoxes. Try to borrow from the future as much as possible. Because the future is also in the present. All time is in every moment of time. When we realize this, we can start to rectify our past."

Oh, wow, I think as it starts to click.

Then, being the good student that I am, I wonder, *What about my past do I need to rectify?*

A surge of the upper world pulses in me as I feel into the future of everything working out. Even though I don't know exactly what it looks like, I find some of that potential gloriousness flushing into this moment.

Maybe, Imogen, you have been here with me all along. Maybe as a part of these decisions. *Maybe the unknown is known and here now?*

My mind folds onto itself like a pretzel that I know I'll want to untangle and chew on later.

"Gratitude, for even the things that are very painful, creates a channel for blessings to manifest and a vessel for things to be revealed," the shaman continues, as I write. "Gratitude activates something profound that can bring you to a state of joy: the healthiest emotion because it is not contingent on appearance but is inherent to you as a soul."

This. Is. Incredible.

I step away from the call reflecting.

I see myself getting through this surgery easily, very much in a state of surrender. I feel like there is a whole world on the other side of it that was entirely inaccessible to me before but is already here and filled with welcome.

Funny, personable, and very much on top of things, my doc is fantastic pre- and post-op. "The surgery went well," she tells Mark. "All margins look clear, and all the tissue looks good and healthy."

Mark waits patiently for me to fully wake up. I am groggy and in so much pain that it feels impossible to move and easiest to keep my eyes closed. I am given oxycodone, which makes me overwhelmingly nauseous, but the pain is still very apparent, and I'm told I can have another oxycodone.

I don't want more, much less to get dressed and be put in a car and driven home, but there is no overnight care here, so I don't have a choice. I feel like my insides have been scraped out of me.

I must've lost at least ten pounds! a part of me says, trying to spark some contentment to combat the pain. (I'll look it up later to discover that only mere ounces of tissue were removed.)

I am allotted the longest possible time—three hours—until they kick me out as politely as possible, and I slump into a wheelchair to get to the car. The whole drive home is agony. I feel every bump, and the sun is much too bright for me. I curl to the side of the front seat and close my eyes tightly, wishing away the long hour ahead, feeling myself into being there already.

My prescribed pain management regimen is to alternate between Tylenol and Advil, using the few oxycodone tablets if necessary. Before surgery, my dad had me get approval from my doc for Toradol, an injectable he had at home, albeit expired, which she did say I could use in place of Advil.

Well, I quickly deem the oxycodone unnecessary and agree to try the Toradol when my dad comes by to check on me later. The injection gives me enough relief to sleep with bearable pain. It's a real Dad-saves-the-day moment.

"I can come back and give you another dose at midnight to help you sleep through the night," he then offers.

"Really?" I ask weakly, wanting to scream, *Yes!!!!* but trying to be considerate of his age and need for sleep himself.

"It's not like I make house calls anymore," he says and laughs. "It would be my pleasure, honey."

"Okay, Dad, then yes, please, and big thank you," I pant out.

When he arrives in the middle of the night, he tells me and Mark that he got out of his car next door and nearly tried to enter the neighbor's house. He also can't hear my response when he asks me how I'm doing because he isn't wearing his hearing aids. We all share in the laughter this brings, and I feel my energy slowly returning.

The next day, I receive a notification with my pathology report: All margins are clear. It is confirmed.

I slowly shuffle my way to the bathroom, then to the sink to wash my hands. I brace myself for a moment there, against the counter. I exhale and feel relief as my eyes meet my own in the mirror.

I am relieved to be on the other side of the surgery.

I am relieved that I am okay.

No cancer was found.

I am relieved that I am healthy and well and that my children are being looked after by my family.

I am relieved that we experienced all the other steps for you, Imogen—for a third child, even—so I could be here now, contentedly.

I can go back to sleep.

As I pad my way back to bed and carefully set myself on the pillows, the incisions make themselves known with sharp stabs at the smallest of turns.

But I notice I feel grateful.

Grateful for what my womb provided me.

Grateful that I am not, indeed, mourning its loss.

And I close my eyes again and rest.

Recovery takes longer than I expect, but I make it through, and it is hard for me not to jump up into action after four weeks of rest.

Our friend, who lost his wife early last year, comes, at last, for a visit. We finally get to embrace and break bread together. While my boys are at school, I sit outside with his son, now seven years old, and watch him jump on our trampoline. I count his jumps with him out loud.

"Four hundred and one, four hundred and two... Wow! Keep going!"

It is chilly out and I am still sore, but when the sun shines down and warms us up, I feel his mom thanking me. Like we are connected by an invisible thread and she is supporting me for going through with this surgery, for showing up here with her son—reminding me that in going through with this, I have saved my own life.

Once I hit my fortieth birthday at the end of June, I feel more of my original pre-mom, precancerous self returning. A self that is creative, has ideas to share and curiosities to indulge. A self I haven't paid much attention to, understandably, in recent years, while worrying about how to get through all the decisions.

After losing first my breast tissue, then you, Imogen, and now my womb—and leaving all the BRCA-related worries behind— I have a newfound energy and capacity for the me beyond my body.

About six months after my surgery, the boys are eager to return to Australia—to swim in the ocean and see the place where we spent so much time and never went back to nearly a year and a half ago. They get a week off of school for Thanksgiving, so we decide—now having been saturated in family gatherings for the past year of holidays—to plan a trip, making it two weeks in total.

What will it be like? I wonder, and Mark wonders.

When we reach out to our friends there to tell them our plans, they are excited to reconnect after our swift departure. And when we arrive, we are all amazed at how much easier *everything* is— for all of us.

The flight doesn't seem as far; the boys have an easy journey and are endlessly excited. We know where to go when we land, and even when our jetlagged navigation skills turn us around in the city and we take the bridge over the harbor instead of the tunnel under it, we easily find our way into Manly.

It rains, but it is warm and it doesn't bother us. We know where to drive to find indoor play spaces, we know where to park to grab groceries outside of the deluge, and we know what stores will deliver any items we forget.

The sun comes out and we all walk to the beach. The boys no longer run off and I no longer shout at them. They are comfortable in the water, like no time has passed, remembering the pathways we used to frequent.

I'm delighted by how much they love seeing their old friends and how quickly they pick up where they left off. I'm shocked to see the *positive* effects COVID actually had on us: giving us a crazy-close bond to those we saw and corroborated with during and after lockdowns, those I showed up for and showed up for me and who are still here.

I feel invigorated to write, Mark works and is energized by his morning swims again in nature's brisk salt water, and the upstairs neighbor of our new Airbnb is super chatty and helpful—embracing the boys and their chaos, effortlessly engaging in conversation.

I'm no longer intimidated by the not-knowing of how it all works here and am reveling in how it is all no longer new to me and how much connection we have with the community in our re-arrival. I'm even able to share a long list of resources with a friend of my brother's, her husband and their two boys, who only arrived a few weeks ago for a few years' stint of their own.

Being back in the US reset us, reset me. There is no longer friction here to face. The boys are thriving and their confidence is growing. They're supported and encouraged.

Knowing all of that and having all of that propels me forward to say, "I think we might move back here," to nearly everyone we see.

"I got chills when you said that," my friend and mom to one of Julian's best mates here says.

"It was so different during COVID—so many stressors. It'd be such a different story if you came back," another encourages.

I'm only a phone call away, I hear my mom's voice in my head, while I'm in the shower later.

I find myself thinking that the boys have such a good sense of their family now and an established connection—plus, they're older—and it'd be so much easier to go back and forth if we returned.

I daydream. I can't help it. The big feeling is back.

Imogen, do you remember when I told you that a psychic once said I might have three kids and live by the sea? She thought that sea could be Cape Cod. But how could she have seen Australia? None of us could have, and yet, here we are.

I still get glimmers of feeling my capacity open up again for you. To say, "Damn the conditions and limitations!"—of even my own body, or lack thereof—when I see or hear of another woman having a child in her forties, handling it all (or so I think). Especially when I've come off a few conflict-free days with the boys.

But then I go in for a blood draw—for something like my cholesterol—and one of the veins above my wrist looks funky, kind of flat and bruised, and the phlebotomist will ask, "Have you had chemo?" as she turns my arm side to side to find the best place for a puncture.

And I will say, "Yes," looking down at that same spot, wondering how I didn't know that weird-looking vein was a tell and grateful I didn't pass such things on to you.

There is still sadness in me for letting you go, Imogen, but are you really gone? Are you really lost?

As I put down my pen to complete our story, I hear you whisper:

"Take care of my brothers, Mommy.
Take care of you.
And remember to love Daddy, too.
I love you."

And that is what I will continue to do. In a life that glitters along the sea. Past, present, and future, all happening now.

Thank you, Imogen.

Thank you.

acknowledgments

To all the BRCA1 carriers out there, I hope this story shows you, most importantly, that BRCA1 is not a barrier to love.

Alle Mudrick: Working in tandem with you is defying gravity. What a thrill! What a gift! To soar together. Thank you for all you do that I can see and all you do that I can't. The ripple effect is extensive, incredible, and enormously appreciated!! Big thank you to Elizabeth Oliver for your eagle-eyes on my proofread, too!

Jamie Kushner Blicher: Thank you thank you thank you for the stunning cover and your willingness to work with me and Third Rail Press. I just love it!

Mary Adkins: You'll see your name on here a few times. Thank you for putting yourself out there and having a podcast and for working with writers. When I had an idea, it landed in the airwaves with what you were selling and became the thing it is today. Thank you for sharing your story, your experiences, and saying yes to me. I have nothing but love and gratitude for you—that keeps coming!

Carol Lin: When we meet in person, I feel like I'm going to

pummel you to the ground like a happy Golden Retriever finding her long-lost companion. You have been fiercely loyal and unendingly encouraging to me, and that energy is returned threefold from my heart to yours. Huge thank you for being virtually by my side as my writer bestie every step of the way, and more, throughout this experience. I cannot wait for what is to come for us.

The Book Incubator: What an incredible program that I'll highly recommend any day to all writers needing a place to start or continue their projects! I wanted connection and support and tools—of which I received in so many wonderful ways. Harrison Gale, Connie Richardson, Joselin Linder, Mary Adkins, and Rufi Thorpe: You all touched my story and helped birth it to life with defined shape and substance. Without you, it certainly wouldn't be what it is today. It might have gotten there eventually, but it's swift launch in full form came at the aid of your hands. Thank you, Emma Dries, for giving me my first edits ever and a PRR very much along the lines of all the direction I'd ever need, and to Lucas Schaefer for reviewing my first synopsis with kindness and care. Thank you to Liz Pickart and Gayle Brown, too, for jumping on board at every opportunity to cheer me on. And to Greg Marshall for highlighting the universality of fertility, regardless of gender.

Thank you to my beta readers and early enthusiasts: Charlie Dixon, Mila Reif, Layla Kajer, Julie Ann Pasquinelli, Sherri McCormick, Mary Adkins, Carol Lin, Kim Danielson, Lisa Joughin, Katherine Emery, and Liza Carpenter. Your feedback and comments throughout my first official draft helped pick me up from the floor and shoot me to the moon to keep going.

Thank you to my later readers, champions and helpers (all so appreciated x a million!) in Australia: Sarah Howie, Amy Hutton, Ariane Beeston, Christine Newell, the 2026 Aus debut crew (including Libby Iriks, Lorena Otes, Lisa Moule, Lauren Novak,

Sophie Stern, Bridie Blake, Leearna Shaw, Katie Hoskins, Josh Hortinela, Jane R. Miles, Tzeyi Koay, Sam Elliott, Cassie Stroud, and Samantha House) and Holly Brunnbauer for introducing us; plus Porscia Lam, Camille Booker, and Louisa Deasey.

To Emma Grey for all you put out into the world: your writing, the gram-o-sphere, and the connections you make with your readers (me!).

So grateful, too, to the inclusivity and warm welcome into my local writing community from fellow authors Laura Irvine, Emma Babbington, Ali Lowe, Maxine Fawcett, Karina May, Vanessa McCausland, Kate Horan, Helen Signy, Claudine Tinellis, and Sandie Docker.

Also, big appreciation for Zibby Owens—as it was learning of you and your endeavors for authors that really lit a fire under me to keep pushing for publication.

Special shout-out to all the authors who read an advanced copy of my story and so generously took the time to provide a blurb (you're the best)! To Bill and Karly at Sound Kitchen in Sydney for their expertise and warm reception of me in recording the audiobook--and to Rebecca Babcock for helping justify the arc of my story in science and logic (I sooo needed that).

Prewriting, I am endlessly grateful for my team of doctors, which starts with my dad. Without you, Dad, I wouldn't have been able to fill in the blanks of IVF and receive the full picture, served up with your generous humor and calm heart to supplement my decisions. It is a gift to be your daughter, to be here—existing on Earth!—and have the scientist side of my brain to ground me in the middle world. To the physicians that made themselves available to me along the way as steady, trustworthy talents and companions, thank you: Mitch Rosen, Wei Wang, Nima Grissom, Gabriel Kind, and Marisa Maroney.

To Brad Satkin, for all you've taught me and the entirety of your being in this world: Thank you.

To my many amazing colleagues who I am also lucky enough to call friends, thank you for all of your support in different impactful ways along my creative and personal journey during this time: Jan Frei, Lisa Falvo-Peckham, Greg Martinez, Greg Rowan, Stephanie Fillbrandt, and Laura and Jay Blumenfeld.

Thank you to my mom for the way you see the world and your unconditional presence, love, and ready-for-any-job superpower + the creative side of my brain and the spiritual side of my heart; to my sister, brother, and your partners, for your support, love and care, and being alongside this journey with me near and far; and for my friends—new and old—for your generosity toward me always. You make being a part of this life so exciting, dynamic, and fun. I love you all.

To my immediate, chosen family—my husband and my children—this story is for you as much as it is for me, for the Imogen who could be, and for our generations to come. I love you more than all my actions could ever portray in any and all possible worlds and forms forever.

www.ingramcontent.com/pod-product-compliance
Lightning Source LLC
Chambersburg PA
CBHW051313130726
47987CB00004B/1778